BAD COLONISTS

The South Seas Letters of Vernon Lee Walker & Louis Becke

❋ NICHOLAS THOMAS AND RICHARD EVES

DUKE UNIVERSITY PRESS   Durham and London, 1999

letter writing is an awful job for me, for I am an awful bad hand at it well! I think that it is time for me to go to bed, & will endeavour to write a little more regularly to you. With love to all

Believe me

Your loving Son.

N. Lee Walker.

Noumea,   February 3rd 1885.

NEW CALEDONIA.

My dear mother.

Ought to beg ashamed of
myself for not writing oftener to you, and have no
excuse to offer except that I am an awfully bad
hand at letter writing. I am afraid that I will
have very little news to tell you.

Believe me
Ever your loving son.
W. Lee Walker.

I wonder when I shall be able to take a trip
home to see you all.
"willie" is in Australia now, but I am afraid that
I will not be able to see him, as Howard will go
to Sydney again, when he arrives their & we cannot
very well, both leave together. Such seems to be
against me.

Three

South Sea

Stories

1. A Truly
Great Man

2. The Doctor's
Wife

3.

W. E. Sparke), wine and spirit merchants, 474½ George st

Walford, Charles W., carpenter, 10 Chester st

Walford, Fred., carpenter, 49 Arthur st

Walford, H., mason, 337 Elizabeth st

Walford, Henry, 75 Albion st

Walford, James, Nelson st, Balmain

Walford, Joseph S., The Retreat, Kennedy st, Glebe

Walford, Margaret, 35 Upper William street S

Walford, W. B., 19 Upper William st N

Walker, J. H. & Son (Henry Walker), flour merchants and biscuit bakers, 168 Sussex st

Walker and Sons, joinery works, Jones st

Walker, —, Rose terrace, Dowling st, Paddington

Walker, —, Turner st, Balmain

Walker, Miss, Harriet, school, 110 Bathurst st

Walker, Rev. Harris, Denison st, Woollahra

Walker, Harry, 2 off Clarence st

Walker, H., Leichhardt st, Glebe

Walker, Henry, Goodlet st

Walker, Henry, cabman, 79 Fig st

Walker, Howard, 73 Lower Fort st

Walker, J. C., law stationer, 91 Elizabeth street

Walker, Mrs. J. E., 128 Queen st, Woollahra

Walker, J. H., Tupper st, Marrickville

Walker, J. P., Temple court, King st

Walker, James, stonemason, Raglan st, Alexandria

Walker, James, Stevens rd, Botany

Walker, James, greengrocer, King st, Balmain

Walker, James, baker, 63 Holt st

Walker, Thomas B., accountant, Nelson's bay rd, Waverley

Walker, Thomas C., draper, Old South Head rd, Paddington

Walker, G. W., barrister, 2 Wentworth court

Walker, G. W., Walker st, St. Leonards

Walker, W. H., Maida, 50 John st, Woollahra

Walker, Watson, Goodhope st, Paddington

Walker, William, painter, Maria st, Marrickville

Walker, Wm., Victoria rd, Marrickville

Walker, W., plasterer, Sarah Ann st

Walker, Wm., Waterloo rd, St. Peters

Walker, W., Westmoreland st, Glebe

Walker, William, engineer, College st, Balmain

Walker, Wm., builder, 267 Crown road

Nanumaga. Ellice Group. S. Pacific
February 21. 1881.

My dear Mama. I have had a rough time of it since last writing
—on the 2ᵗ of this month my station was destroyed by a hurricane.

Island of Peru, Kingsmill Groups.
Sept 24. 1881

S. Lat 1. 20 E Lon 176. 21

My dear Mama. I am sorry that I have nothing but bad, bad news
for you as regards myself for we were castaway on this island on the 24th
of August last and I lost all I possessed in the world. After my last letter

and I have now been laid with it five months, otherwise I am
in good health. don't forget to write to Auckland care of H & M
if I don't come up in the "Geo Noble" to Sydney and with
sincere love to all at home I am dear Mama your affectionate
Son Louis S. Becker.

© 1999 Duke University Press
All rights reserved
Printed in the United States of America on acid-free paper ∞
Typeset in New Baskerville by Tseng Information Systems, Inc.
Library of Congress Cataloging-in-Publication Data appear
on the last printed page of this book.
Research and editorial work on this book were supported by
the Centre for Cross-Cultural Research, an Australian Research
Council Special Research Centre at the Australian National
University. www.anu.edu.au/culture

Extracts from letters by Vernon Lee Walker, Noumea, July 29, 1884, February 3, 1885, and February 3, 1885. Rhodes House Library; photographs courtesy Pacific and Asian History, Research School of Pacific and Asian Studies, Australian National University, Canberra. (pages iv, v, vi)

"Three South Sea Stories," title illustration by B. E. Minns for stories by Louis Becke, *Bulletin,* 16 December 1893, p. 22. National Library of Australia, Canberra. The artist, Benjamin Minns, was a prominent cartoonist and painter of indigenous subjects. (page vii)

Advertisement for McLean Bros. and Rigg, Vernon Lee Walker's sometime employer, from *Sands & McDougall's Directory of Melbourne,* 1878, p. xlii. National Library of Australia, Canberra. (page viii)

Listing from *Sand's Sydney Directory for 1883,* p. 515. National Library of Australia, Canberra. (page ix)

Hiapo, Niuean bark cloth, 180 × 196 cm. Louis Becke made little mention in his writings of the material culture and art of the Pacific, but did collect some pieces, including this one, which he sold to the Technological Museum in Sydney in 1892. He claimed in his letter to J. H. Maiden, then that institution's director, that the "specimens of native cloth" were "among the best ever made on Savage Island." He was paid £12 for the collection, part of which, including this piece, was subsequently transferred to the Australian Museum. Photograph by J. Fields/Nature Focus (Australian Museum). (page x)

Niuean fish hooks, pearl-shell, twine. These pieces were also collected by Becke and sold as part of the same lot to the Technological Museum, later the Museum of Applied Arts and Sciences, and now the Powerhouse Museum. These were exhibited as part of the Powerhouse's "Pirating the Pacific" exhibition in 1993. Reproduced courtesy of the Trustees of the Museum of Applied Arts and Sciences, Sydney. (page xi)

Extracts from letters by Louis Becke, Nanumaga, Ellice Group, South Pacific, February 21, 1881 and Island of Peru, Kingsmill Group, September 24, 1881, first page and final page. Mitchell Library, State Library of New South Wales, Sydney. (pages xii, xiii)

❧ Contents

This book is a work of experimental history, stimulated by the critical anthropology of colonial cultures and by reflective writings on history making. It explores two areas. The first is not so much the fashioning of colonial masculine identities in the disorderly situation of the periphery, but the *failure* or degeneration of coherent selfhood in tropical situations beyond civility. The second is the significance of personal letters as vehicles for self-fashioning. Letters are vital cultural documents, not only as historical sources in the conventional sense, but as artifacts of selfhood, sometimes expressions of the failure of selfhood.

These questions are here explored through two sets of letters, each from traders in the South Pacific in the last quarter of the nineteenth century; we have used the term of the period, "the South Seas," to evoke the region as a theater of European romance and violence, more than as the domain of indigenous imagining and action. This book is about colonists' fantasies and realities rather than those of indigenous people. It is one-sided for methodological reasons, because these particular sets of sources strongly provoke questions concerning the self-making of admittedly obscure colonial actors, although they are not especially revealing so far as indigenous practices, histories, and perceptions are concerned. But our frame of reference does not aim to deny indigenous agency; indigenous realities erupt into these colonial texts and into the lives of their writers, in one case to a fatal degree.

Both series of letters describe not colonial triumphs on the part of white men secure in their superior identities, but fraught circumstances in which not only the respectability and integrity of the writers, but even their racial identity, become questionable. Both series of letters were addressed to the writers' mothers, and there are comparable silences. One set is from Vernon Lee Walker, an unfortunate and unsuccessful character otherwise scarcely known to the historical record, whose self-account is full of poignancy. The other is from Louis Becke, once a best-selling writer, one still well-known to students of Australian and Pacific literature and the literature of colonial expansion. Becke's best stories, some of them based on the experiences related in these previously unpublished letters, rank with works such as

Robert Louis Stevenson's *The Ebb-Tide* and Jack London's *South Sea Tales,* and similarly convey the violence and degeneracy of colonial life in the Pacific frankly and powerfully.

This book is not a conventional scholarly edition of these letters. Rather, it exemplifies what could be seen as an undeveloped genre of critical and reflective scholarship. Rather than being an exhaustive edition that provides some balanced contextualization, we have framed these texts in a partial way, making their interest from particular angles apparent. Yet we have also aimed to present them in their integrity, in a fashion that draws attention not only to the peculiar fascination of sources that may be inconsequential, from the perspective of a global colonial history, but to their specificity. They are not simply texts or historical documents, but writings and indeed artifacts of a particular kind. Being letters, they raise wider questions about what letters actually are, how they work as powerful but awkward instruments in social relations that do not merely communicate information or reflect existing statuses, but often say both too little and too much. Letters vitally animate the business of reciprocal self-fashioning, and reflect the real lapses, and crises, of self-fashioning that are much in evidence on the colonial periphery. The issue of degeneration—of civilized, or racially specific, selves—figures prominently in the literature of the period, in psychology, anthropology, and biology as well as in more extravagant forms in fiction. The relation between Becke's own correspondence and his stories is of great interest in this context.

The letters are suggestive, also, about the relationships between popular literature and obscure personal notes, between public and private, and between ideology and self-perception. Self-fashioning has become a popular theme in literary studies in recent years, but these letters remind us forcefully that this is more than a literary effort; however powerfully self-fashioning is expressed in writing, it is also something that had to be *done,* by particular people in particular situations—for better or worse.

This is a multiauthored book in more senses than usual. Readers will note differences of voice and style between different essays and commentary sections. Because we broadly share a stance regarding the sources we are engaging with, we have avoided signaling on the contents page or within the text itself who wrote what, but some readers may find it helpful to know that the introduction, chapter 1, and the epilogue were written by Nicholas Thomas and chapters 3 and 5 by Richard Eves; the commentary on the Walker letters is by Thomas and that on Becke by Eves.

❋ Acknowledgments

Vernon Lee Walker's letters of 1875–1882, of which we reproduce only a few in this volume, are in the State Library of Victoria, Melbourne, Australia; those covering the period 1883–1887, all published here, are in Rhodes House, Oxford, England. Louis Becke's letters form part of a collection of his manuscripts and memorabilia in the State Library of New South Wales, Sydney, Australia. We are grateful to these institutions for permission to publish these documents here. Christine Dureau transcribed Vernon Lee Walker's letters for Nicholas Thomas in 1990–91. Some of the material appeared in Thomas's book, *Colonialism's Culture* (1994). Danielle Banks did further proofing and editorial work for this full publication in late 1996. On this project, as well as many others, Jennifer Newell has provided exemplary editorial support. We must thank Stephen Eisenman, who was at one stage thinking of calling his important new book on Gauguin *Bad Colonist;* when it became *Gauguin's Skirt* he graciously allowed us to use what seemed an irresistible title.

Nicholas Thomas would like to thank Margaret Jolly, and the many colleagues and friends with whom he has discussed questions of colonial culture in many places over the past decade. This book owes a great deal to those conversations.

Richard Eves wishes to thank Roe Sybylla for her unending support and encouragement, both intellectual and moral, during the writing of this project.

We would both like to thank Ken Wissoker at Duke University Press for his encouragement.

In the epoch of the word-processed letter, the fax, and the e-mail message it is easy to think of the letter as a text rather than an artifact. This is how letters have long been used by historians. Official or personal, they are collections of words, of evidence. The letter attests to the event, the attitude, or the shifting psyche of the biographer's subject. Letters are evaluated: Was the writer a witness to what is described, or was the account merely hearsay? The historian supplants the original recipient and takes the information that the writer had to give. Whether historians or not, we all use letters in this way: to convey some business information, to keep in touch with a friend, to hear of a death.

Letters indeed communicate, but they do other things and are other things. Most of all they are objects. They are deceptively ubiquitous. They just lie around, eluding reflection, while bearing peculiarly manifold features: the thickness of the paper, the manner of folding, the size and type of the envelope, the unusual stamps. There is the tangibility and the awkwardness and all the personality of the handwriting: the inky presence of the absent person. There is the necessity of the signature, the raggedness of an enclosed newspaper cutting. There is the envelope that appears to have been tampered with, but has in fact been torn open because a correspondent remembered something that needed to be added, or was struck by anxiety and had to subtract or replace a page.

This materiality is something that the historian tends not to come clean about. On the one hand we all experience the excitement of what seems to be a direct encounter with a past actor, and this is most provoking when the actor, the writer, is (in the most vulgar case) a famous person. It may be still more exciting if the person is not famous but remarkable, if his or her epistolic testament constitutes a personal discovery, a discovery for research. This is the moment at which the researcher—you or I—revels in the privilege of scholarship. We are often in archives that are not open to simply anybody; it is the fact of our doctoral research, our Ph.D., our seriousness of whatever sort, that constitutes the ticket, and even then the librarians may be standoffish, they may hesitate before they bring out certain sorts of material, they may insist on white gloves, pencils, and old wooden bookrests for heavy volumes. Still, here we are, in Rhodes House, or the Mitchell, or the Petherick Room. One's fellow readers seem to range from obsessives to eccentrics; there are involuntary, anxious gestures suggesting anticipation and frustration, but not much noise apart from a slight clatter in the keyboard of somebody's laptop, the rapid movements of one's neighbor's pencil, the insufficiently hushed chatter of the desk staff. This is the moment: the materials appear from some subterranean stack, we are undoing a faded pink ribbon, rummaging through a file, and taking these pieces of paper out of a succession of envelopes. Some sheets are heavy, stiff, and curiously clean, considering that their writing took place on a small cargo boat, perhaps on deck in fine weather. Others are delicate, blue, of what I think of as airmail paper, the blue ink insufficiently distinct. Then there is the magic of the script: the missionary's bold flourish and the awkward, unpracticed hand of the trader. In the 1880s an inconsequential racist has exposed an extraordinary life, and it is all too tactile. You begin to read; it is some time before you are accustomed to the hand and the odd little devices that stand in for punctuation. The letters do not so much communicate as suggest mysteries and a strangely wild colonial life. You keep reading, and the place is suddenly closing; the laptops have been put to sleep, the eccentrics are shuffling off, the staff are impatient to get you out.

Much more could be written about the power and the magic of the archive; this is a theme that has been addressed by Greg Dening, Natalie Davis, and Ann Stoler, among others. Though the peculiar scene and situation of letter reading needs to be acknowledged, our interest here is more in the letter as an artifact, as a composed artifact, and as a technique. We are mainly concerned with personal letters, though official, legal, and business letters are artifacts too, which discover all kinds of ways of contriving their gravity. Personal letters, and most particularly those from intimates, are, we might hazard, inherently poignant. They do not simply suggest or imply distance and loss, but attempt to defeat spatial separation by producing presence; they make absence present. We understand the letter not simply as a piece of writing, but as an embodied expression, as an element of what Marilyn Strathern (1988) identifies as the "partible person." A person's script is his or her "hand," it is a distributed aspect of his or her self, that renders the absence of the whole all the more painful: insofar as the letter succeeds it fails, because it only evokes more forcefully the person who is in fact not there, in person. These textual artifacts, however, always work toward some negotiation of this failure; letters sustain relationships more or less unsatisfactorily, despite and across distance. Yet there may be circumstances in which letters do not aim to defeat space so much as exploit it. We all know that there are things that are easier to say and do in writing than face-to-face. Distancing is itself action, action that creates autonomy, that may be imagined to enable the definition of self in spaces beyond the ties of kinship, conjugality, and tradition. Robinson Crusoe, most particularly in Ian Watt's insightful reading (1957: 65ff), prefigures the accomplishment of colonial self-fashioning in this sense. But the colonists discussed here are no Crusoes.

If letters often sustain relationships in the absence of face-to-face meetings, those relationships are not simply perpetuated without modification. Letters can also be stages for declarations, through which one's connection with another person may be intensified, fashioned, disfigured, or ended. Stories begin, turn, and end with letters. A whole book could be—for all I know, has been—written about letters in Western art and the narratives they figure. Surely their most brilliant deployment, their most obscurely suggestive appearances, are in Vermeer's paintings. His women receive, read, and write epistles intently, with absorption, sometimes with a flutter of anxiety, the delicious agitation of passion, probably the fraught play of adultery.

If letters initiate, reaffirm, or change social relationships, they always evoke the association between sender and recipient in a particular way— by being formal or familiar, by being deferential or assertive. This may be simple and relatively uninteresting if both parties to a correspondence perceive their association in the same way, but constructions may differ or may be contested, depending on a political, or micropolitical, field. I may strike you as offhand, or I may assume a familiarity that you find inappropriate. "Do not write to me as 'my dearest Dr Mabel Palmer.' 'Dear Dr Palmer' is quite enough," insisted a feminist and liberal in South Africa in 1951. She was writing to Lily Moya, the young Xhosa woman whose education she was supporting.

> now for more personal matters, which it is even more difficult to speak about, but which I also feel must be made plain.
>
> You say that one of your reasons for wishing to be in Durban is that you wish to see more of me, but have you ever asked yourself whether I wish to see more of you? As a matter of fact I do not. Your romantic and self-centred imagination has built up for you a picture in which you are to be my devoted and intimate friend. Now you must forgive

me for saying that this is nonsense. Even if you were a European girl of your age it would still be all nonsense. What basis of companionship could there be between a quarter educated girl of eighteen and an experienced old lady like myself? And of course the racial situation in Durban makes all these things more difficult. (In Marks 1987: 136)

In her remarkable letters, Moya had attempted to fashion a close if maternalistic association, which is here fairly cruelly ruled out by Palmer. This typifies the way in which letters take risks; they can also work to seduce or disguise seduction, and may conceal or obscure as much as they convey and disclose, as they so often do in the great epistolic novels, like Richardson's *Clarissa*. As practices, as artifacts that have lives in their composition and consumption, letters are often highly charged; their writing and reading may be marked by tears, felt pain, and certainly often anxiety.[1]

A letter may be a vehicle for a struggle with another person, a struggle for his or her good estimation, or it may simply reaffirm friendship. But it may also provide the opportunity for an effort of self-definition. If many activities, such as dressing and cooking, figure as everyday contexts for working out what kind of person one is, letters of any substance or consequence not only constitute another such context, but surely one that is peculiarly intense: through style, content, graphic gesture, maybe even tears, one says who one is. If this is so, to some degree, of letters from whatever place or period, it is true in a heightened way for colonial letters. Many of those who left Europe for Africa, the "East," or the Pacific did so for many years, if not for good. Under these circumstances, the letter is quite different from the holiday letter, the love letter, or one written during a brief separation. In those instances, the relationship at issue has another life in meetings, transactions, or domesticity. Though gifts of artifacts, colonial souvenirs, or cash that might be sent through the post had their own significance, letters were central to the reproduction of the colonist's kinship and familial ties. Whereas a particular identity as a son or sister is usually made through diverse actions—shared work and worship, sociality, gifts, rebukes—the absent colonist's relationships, if they were to endure at all, had to be sustained through writing. A colonist might be, or might try to be, a master in practice, and might dominate those around him or her brutally; yet, when he or she wrote home, that act of writing could only proceed around distance and lack. We are not arguing that colonists should retrospectively be accorded some compassion that critical scholarship has tended to deprive them of.

This book presumes a critical stance toward colonial racism but has little interest in the reiteration of generalized condemnation. Intellectual, and perhaps political, progress on this front can only proceed through the specification of various state and other racisms, and through the tracing of their cultural genealogies and institutional and practical expressions (cf. Stoler 1995). This book contributes to this project in a modest way, in drawing attention to the contradictory workings of racial and colonial self-estimations in peripheral situations. We aim to draw attention to the incompleteness that is almost intrinsic to settler identity, that renders it incomplete, and that is chronically negotiated, and peculiarly exhibited, in the practice of correspondence.

Letters were almost the sole channel through which personal relationships could be maintained, and it is accordingly not surprising to find Vernon Lee Walker "most fearfully disappointed at not getting any letters from home," soon after he arrived in Melbourne from England, "for I had been looking out all the week for the mail" (February 8, 1876). Correspondence was also the vital nexus through which contact with metropolitan society in a wider sense persisted, less so for a settler in one of the Australian cities than for a planter days away from other whites in remote parts of Fiji or the Solomon Islands. In these latter cases, where there was limited access to other sources of knowledge such as newspapers, individual correspondence was still more crucial. Some sustained it and some did not. In the course of the first series of letters published here, Vernon Lee Walker moves across this spectrum of locations: he is at first in the entirely urban domains of Melbourne and Sydney. We do not reproduce all his lettters from this period, though some of them foreshadow his isolation and uncertainty; we hear of his frustrations as a commercial traveler, albeit a prosperous one; he then moves to Noumea, and, as the bright prospects of his brother's business diminish, he is finally running a small plantation and trading in unpacified areas of the then New Hebrides (now Vanuatu). Over this succession of moves, the question of self-estimation and identity becomes steadily more central and more fraught in his writing.

All too often, letters come back to what Greg Dening has called the erotics of writing, in the sense of a highly charged play of written desires and silences. Often, they are quite literally animated by sex, by marital infidelity, and (in the colonial situation) by the racial and cultural infidelity of miscegenation. Just as letters are produced out of absence—for the most part one would not write if one was present—they are often energized by loud silences and awkward absences, by detours around the spaces that are problematic, by statements that conceal more than they disclose. Insofar as sexuality surfaces in Walker's letters it is as an absence, sometimes a conspicuous one, certainly a predictable one, given that these are, after all, addressed to his mother, yet nevertheless a perplexing one, if you are as curious about historical characters as I tend to be.

It is odd not even to have an engraving or a photograph. Mostly, when one does research on an individual, there is some visual image that can flit about in the back of one's mind. This is an index of the extent to which historical research is engaged mostly with people of consequence, people important enough to be sketched or painted. Hence I can form an image of Becke, though it derives from a photograph that substantially postdates the correspondence published here. In the case of unimportant Walker, there is nothing to go on but his own writing, and he never describes himself—why would he, to his mother?—except to inform her—to disturb her, I imagine—that his skin has darkened. In the absence of an image, I imagine a thin man, a gaunt version of the type in a Boys' Own story, but it is a hazy image, and not one that ever has a secure presence in my effort to visualize this sometime clerk, storeman, and trader.

If many letters are primarily about the relationship between writer and recipient, this is less obviously the case for Walker and his mother (we have no sense of how she responded and wrote back to him). Though, certainly, the letters are half-hearted efforts to sustain contact (they are mostly written around Christmas, when familial ties or their waning were no doubt on his mind), what is more conspicuous is Walker's effort to create and fix his own social location. But he is a bad colonist, not in the sense that he is powerful enough to be evil, to exploit any number of people in any especially grievous way, but in the sense that he is bad at being one, bad at imagining himself as someone shouldering the white man's burden, as evoking a coherent or legitimate selfhood through his own script, through any imperial script he has made his own.

Correspondence forces a matching, or mutual, assessment of the two dimensions of the white colonizer's identity—his or her roots in a "civilized" country and his or her location as a pioneer in a place of settlement. Writers from geographically remote situations would normally, as a matter of course, give an account of themselves. In the colonial situation, this accounting involved an effort to distill, out of the plethora of experience and response, a particular imagining of being, place, and future prospects, which would be projected in relation to expectations about what mother or relatives at home wanted to know—or should be forced to know. Colonialism did not happen simply by virtue of economic transactions or military intrusions; it was also something that had to be imagined and narrated, not just in mass-circulation missionary magazines, administrators' memoirs, or official reports, but also in the minds of particular people whose inscriptions of colonial identity might obviously differ from published, authorized renderings. The imaginative dimension may be most conspicuous in representations that celebrated empire and progress: in the intertwining of social or racial evolutionary ideas with legitimations of rule over backward races, or in the strong current of utopianism in nineteenth-century settler colonialism that saw new societies, not simply as extensions of the metropolitan nation that might aspire to reproduce its civility, but also as better, cleaner, or more vigorous forms, composed either of uplifted natives or a race of tough pioneers. These letters tell another tale.

1 ❀ "An Awfully Bad Hand at Letter Writing":
Vernon Lee Walker and Colonial History

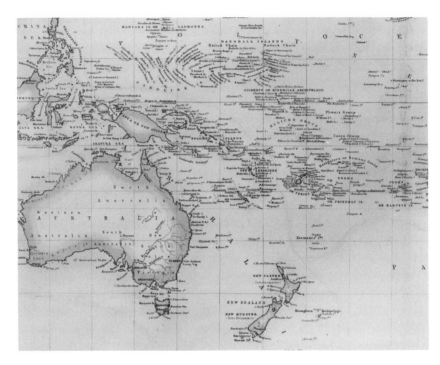

Detail from J. Hugh Johnson, "Oceania, or Islands in the Pacific Ocean, on Mercators projection, comprising Polynesia, Malaysia and Australasia." Engraved by A. Fullarton & Co. Edinburgh/London, 1862. Plate 71 from *The Royal Illustrated Atlas of Modern Geography*. National Library of Australia, Canberra.

Vernon Lee Walker wrote to his mother from Melbourne, from Sydney, from Noumea, and from small trading boats between the New Hebrides (now Vanuatu) and New Caledonia. This was the period of the most conspicuously rapacious stage of European expansion: the scramble for Africa. The last of his letters overlaps with Stanley's expeditions into the Congo, although Walker was dead before the triumph of those journeys was established, before *In Darkest Africa* was published in 1890. It is difficult to avoid the view, however, that that book, a model of aggressive pioneering masculinity, would not have helped Walker much. While Stanley epitomized the success of colonialism at its most confident moment, Walker's world was inhabited by failed businesses, bad creditors, and recalcitrant and aggressive natives.

You might wonder why the fragmented and semiliterate notes that constitute Walker's correspondence deserve publication. Though his sentences were composed at the height of what global historians would call the imperial age, they derive from the most peripheral journeys and incidents, from petty trading and planting in fringe colonies. Though he writes about conflicts between islanders and traders, and incidentally about young Pacific port towns, now capitals in Fiji and New Caledonia, with their rawness and desperate façades of civility, there are many other sources, and many other published accounts, that are often far more detailed, that tell us about daily life in Suva and Noumea or the routines and irregularities of the trade in indentured labor from the New Hebrides and the Solomons to the sugar plantations of Queensland and Fiji.[1] What we have here are merely passing glimpses.

Walker's time was a transitional one. The Pacific had changed a great deal since the early nineteenth century, when there were beachcombers—resident castaways or deserters—in the islands but virtually no settlers, and indigenous people remained almost fully in control of their own resources. Islanders, moreover, generally retained the capacity to define the terms of exchange with those who sought sandalwood and provisions, they resisted missionary intrusions or allowed them voice and space on emphatically indigenous terms, and they sustained their theaters of ritual and nonritual

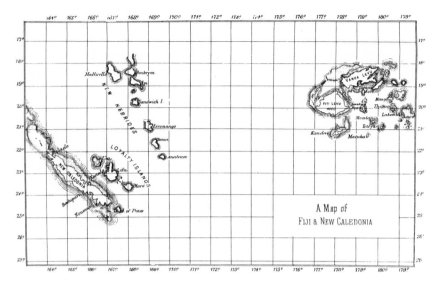

"A Map of Fiji and New Caledonia," from J. W. Anderson, *Notes of Travel in Fiji and New Caledonia with some remarks on South Sea Islanders and their Languages,* London: Ellissen, 1880. National Library of Australia, Canberra.

violence as it suited them. The whites who crossed the beach to deal with islanders accommodated themselves to indigenous relations and gambits more than they imposed their own. From the 1840s onward, however, trading and missionary activities increased steadily, though quite unevenly. In the eastern Pacific, British Protestant missions were well established early in the century, and the French were playing colonialists from the 1840s. In Fiji, a tiny European beachcomber settlement had expanded dramatically in the 1860s as colonists tried to capitalize on a cotton boom caused by the American Civil War. There were suddenly thousands rather than hundreds of whites in the islands, who created new trading relations and interisland trading relations based on the demand for laborers as well as provisions and commodities. New Caledonia had been annexed by the French as a penal colony in 1853, and in subsequent decades traders and planters became active in parts of the New Hebrides and the Solomon Islands. The intensified activity that extended well beyond the secure European enclaves provoked a good deal of conflict, which led the colonial powers to assume control in Fiji in 1874, in the Solomon Islands from 1893, and in the New Hebrides in 1907. In the 1870s and 1880s, much trade and labor migration was taking place and port towns were emerging, but the reach of colonial government was decidedly limited. In the regions in which Walker was active as a trader, there was no formal control and certainly no administration. There were occasional and generally half-hearted efforts to investigate allegations of white misbehavior, and less restrained punitive actions against indigenous perpetrators of "outrages" against whites. In general, though, this was a time of unofficial colonialism, of commercial expansion—and sporadic contraction—that was unlicensed or marginally licensed by the state.

Walker was once alluded to in print by a journalist but not named, and this is emblematic of the extent to which unimportant colonists such as he, and ordinary people most of the time, have had negligible or nonexistent capacities to establish a presence in print, a citation, a documentary trace. And, though he is by no means inarticulate, the style and punctuation of his letters make it evident that writing was something of a labor and a strain. Are we, in publishing his letters and giving his account of himself and his uncertainty greater circulation than he would ever have anticipated, pushing further the effort of social historians to bestow voices upon the poor, on ordinary people, on women, on marginal and oppressed groups? Such work has supplanted the grand traditions of elitist history and done away with its pretension that the world was made by generals and members of parliament and colonial governors. It has shown that common people are not just recipients of benefits from above or victims of dominance, but actors who make themselves and have their own cultures and vitality, their hidden means of survival and resistance. That sort of history has been a liberal or left-wing project, and has mostly been motivated by sympathetic identifications and by a sense that the histories of minorities and oppressed groups were suppressed or stolen—as though they were substantial things available to be recuperated and restored.

It is not possible to empathize or identify with Vernon Lee Walker in this way. His story is poignant, and there may be moments when one feels his loneliness and sense of hopelessness. But he was not a member of some dominated group that a radical history would want to retrospectively validate. If we describe him as an inconsequential racist, we would not merely be capitalizing rhetorically on the ideological differences between the late nineteenth century and the end of the twentieth; in one sense, virtually all white people, and certainly most colonizers, of that time could be considered racists from our notionally enlightened vantage point. There is a certain facility in such identifications, too easy self-congratulation and too easy summation of different ways of identifying people who, of course, often were racist. But the point about Walker is different. By the lights of his time, within the spectrum of views then held, his attitudes toward Pacific islanders were harsh, frank, and bigoted. He used the word "nigger" more readily than others did (though probably not more readily than others of his class); he used it to apply to Fijians at a time when Europeans (or at least elite Europeans) generally referred to them as "natives" or as "Fijians," when fascination with past cannibalism was fused uneasily with appreciative responses to the etiquette and civility of Fijian chiefs and to the carvings, barkcloths, and pottery that were already being manufactured, not just for their local usefulness and value, but also for tourists and handicraft shows. Though his feelings toward islanders shift, the most he can do is express affection for individual servant boys. He does not, of course, articulate any theory of racial difference and does not venture opinions about whether people such as the Fijians and the New Caledonian "canaques" are permanently and irreducibly inferior to whites or whether they are potentially to be civilized and converted to Christianity. His comments on islanders embody a plurality of responses and attitudes; he is repelled, occasionally amused, and confident of his capacity to sustain control: "I never trust one of them, & always treat them fairly, the consequence is that I can do with natives, more than any one else." This range of responses finds the native in turn quaint, odd, dangerous, and disgusting and is broadly consistent with the observations of more articulate racist writers of the time who rejected missionary and philanthropic humanism.

If Walker cannot be produced here, as a character and as a writer, as somebody to be identified with or someone who in some sense seems to have been unjustly forgotten by historical memory (as if there were not innumerable others), it may instead be his very failure and lack of consequence that is important to us, that makes these letters not just legible, but maybe vital reading from the point of view of current concerns to reassess the nature and effect of colonial histories in both colonizing and colonized cultures.

The confidence of colonialism in the epoch of Stanley was not simply military and economic, but also epistemic: it was expressed, and to some extent made possible, by an attitude toward prospectively possessed spaces, toward geography, that was both cartographic and aesthetic. Terrain could be described and known; in an obvious sense, an awareness of possible routes, resources, settlements, and points of control were requirements of colonial government and trade. The full and precise accounting of topography that was realized in charts and surveys also afforded a kind of intellectual security that implied a corresponding pervasiveness of vision and dominance. Observations on the character and majesty of shorelines or rugged hills are so frequent in exploratory and travel literature that they seem as natural as the features represented—standard elements of the landscape of the genre. But appreciations of countryside are never innocent of wider narratives and implications that especially concern property. Images and stories of colonization, in particular, are likely to conflate different kinds of belonging: the land rightly belongs to those who feel that they belong to it. As Bernard Smith has observed, "The European control of the world required a landscape practice that could first survey and describe, then evoke in new settlers an emotional engagement with the land that they had alienated from its aboriginal occupants" (1985: ix; see also Mitchell 1994). Smith is referring here to visual representations and painting in particular, but writing about topography can work possessively in the same way, through a similar range of scientific, aesthetic, or sentimental registers. In addition, evocative writing about landscapes and scenery may be less concerned with establishing possession than transposing exploratory or pioneering journeys from a mundane to an almost divine level, instilling higher purpose and legitimacy: "On returning for the third time to the Nyanza, in January, 1889, and during our long stay at Kavalli for two and a half months, it was unseen, until suddenly casting our eyes, as usual, towards that point where it ought to be visible, the entire length of the range burst out of the cloudy darkness, and gratified over a thousand pairs of anxious eyes that fixed their gaze upon the singular and magnificent scene" (Stanley 1890: ii, 291–92).

Though there is great variety in modes of geographical observation —some extravagant and lyrical, some more contracted and mundane— all manifestations, like all transactions between colonizers and indigenous peoples, were implicated in the larger project of European apprehension and control to which Smith refers. At the same time, a place much closer to Walker's sphere of activity, also at the colonial periphery, could be responded to in these terms: "What a lovely spot! Along the coast in both directions stretches the thick fringe of coco-nut palms; behind them the deep green of the virgin forest. . . . Around us is the pale blue water of the lagoon" (Woodford 1890: 147). This is banal, and not much less so at the time than for readers numbed since by tourist clichés. What is striking, though, is that Walker scarcely engages in this sort of description. He does express his astonishment as he beholds the scenery of New Zealand; and he does go into raptures of a sort concerning the settler paradise of Mago (Mango) in Fiji (though what he celebrates in this case is less the natural environment than the exemption from labor the colonists appear to enjoy). During his Pacific travels, however, despite the fact that he is writing home, to a mother unfamiliar with the Pacific, he makes virtually no effort to evoke lagoons or beaches or mountains. He does talk about having to walk miles over coral and about traveling up and down a river, but the landscape is referred to rather than depicted; it does not emerge as an object of spectacle, as something detached from particular transits or uses. This failure epitomizes one of the critical senses in which he is, as he says, "an awfully bad hand at letter writing." Given the larger significance of remarks upon scenery, his shortcomings can be considered, not merely in terms of some basic ineptitude in the art of composition, but as part of a wider failure in the art of colonization, and specifically a failure on Walker's part to fashion himself, to write himself up as a confident colonial actor, whose particular ventures form part of a rounded aesthetic, economic, and political endeavor.

This signals the extent to which a perception of colonialism based on figures such as Stanley is an incomplete perception. Walker's letters show that even at the moment at which imperialism must have seemed globally triumphant, before it entered the cycles of depression and warfare that culminated in the First World War and before the unity of the British Empire was threatened and then undone by Boer nationalism in South Africa—even at_ this moment, there was an incoherence to settler identity, a perception, inadequately articulated, that the products of the rough life were no longer suitable for society at home. So far from uplifting others, the trader lapsed into his own kind of savagery. Much of the colonial writing of this period is optimistic, blandly self-assured, absurd in retrospect. Walker's letters register something very different. The most famous articulation of this vision came later, at the turn of the century, in Conrad's *Heart of Darkness,* and subsequently, pessimistic and radical writing that exposed the corruption of colonization emerged from many parts of the empire; but Walker's letters show us something that the brilliance and coherence of Conrad's prose could only disguise: the way in which a failure of colonialism was manifested in a failure of writing, in an awfully bad hand.

Little is known of Walker's life other than what can be discerned from his letters. We have avoided annotating them in a conventional way, which would tell you what little we know about which ships he traveled on, more about the individuals he refers to in passing, and so on. That contextualization and specification is normally the business of an editor of historical texts of this kind. The information is supposed to make particular sources more accessible and useful, to install them like museum relics in a well-illuminated cabinet. It is not clear to us that knowing more about Walker's accounts or relatives would somehow make this correspondence into a valuable component of "the" historical record. Admittedly, such details supply certain facts for those concerned with, for example, the incidents of violence that led to extension of colonial control in the area and the failure of small Australian businesses in the Pacific. We are not opposed to that sort of annotation in principle and have done it in other texts. But in this case such worthy scholarship would seem to miss the point: the "evidence" here lies less in what Walker reports than in his haziness, in his inability to report, in the anxiety and epistemic murk his bad hand ironically renders so intelligible.

January 19*th* 1878
Melbourne.

Dear mother,

I suppose that you will have guessed that I have been to Fiji, as I did not write to you by the last mail.[1] I did not know myself that I was going until the steamer was starting.

I went down to Sandridge to see them all off, and just as we were saying good-bye, Mr Thompson said that I had better come, and that Mr Renwick would make it all right with Mr Rigg. So, after a little persuasion, I thought that I could not do better than go, since I knew that I would never get another trip like it again. Away, I went with no clothes but what I had on my back, however I managed all right as between Mr Thompson and Howard, I got clothes enough to last me till I got there.

We left Melbourne on Thursday evening at six o-clock, and cleared through Melbourne heads at half past ten, we ought to have remained at anchor inside the heads, as it is dangerous going through at night, but since Mr Thompson was in a hurry to get away, by tipping the pilot a little extra we got through all right. Directly we were through rough weather commenced, which continued more or less till we got to "Suva." Every-one was sick except Mr Thompson and myself. However on the following Sunday, it came on to blow a gale, and the knocking about was something awfull, so much so, that it was rather too much for me, and I was sick all day. Strange to say ever afterwards directly I awoke, I was sick, although I was all right directly afterwards; I fancy that it must have been through the sea air getting in my mouth, and filling it full of salt.

Church was out of the question this Sunday as everyone was so ill, and it was so rough it was almost impossible to sit down. Howard was too ill to move out of his cabin, and I got the steward to lash a

Sydney N.S.W.
December 18th/83.

My dear mother.

I was pleased to find a letter lying on
my desk, from you when I came in to the office the
other morning=
I have no foreign note paper in the office, and this is the only
sheet I can rake up, and it is not as clean as it might be=
Howard has at last got a house, strange to say it is in
the same terrace where I am living, which will be handy
For a house in town, it is the best situation you could wish
for, the front view is looking right down the harbour,
and from the back you look right up the Parramatta
river, there is always a cool breeze, and very few mosquitoes
It is now being papered & painted & I do not suppose that
they will get into it till the middle of January.
The only objection to it is the approach as you have to
pass through the part of the town where the chinamen
live, and the smell of their cooking is not always the
sweetest; omnibusses however pass the door every three
minutes so that you need never walk=
We are getting into the warm weather now, and we have
had one or two very hot days.
Howard has had a lot of trouble lately, the last
was the death of our agent in Noumea (Mr William
He was a most particular friend of Howards, and had
splendid prospects before him = The poor fellow was getting

on to his horse, when the horse shied, and threw him, on to
his head. He was on 31 years of age and leaves a wife and
three children, his wife only being confined about three day
before the accident=

Howard, Lowe, & myself are dining with a Mrs Mossitter on
Christmas day, you may be sure that we shall not forget
you at home.= I am not going out of town for the
holidays, and do not know what I shall do to pass
away the time=

We are very busy in the office day as we are two hands short!
one being on the sick, & one away for a fortnights holiday
Mr Rigg of McLean Bros & Rigg died last Sunday and
is to be buried to day, he has left a number of friends behind
him, and will be greatly missed=

I fancy that I owe Cyril a letter tell him, tell him
that I will most likely answer it during the holidays, I am
such an awful bad correspondent, and there is no news
of any interest to those at home=

I am rather late in wishing you a Merry Christmas, but
I trust that you will have a Happy & Prosperous New
year. Hoping that all are well at home

            Believe me, my dear mother
              Your loving son.
                V. Lee Walker

Letter by Vernon Lee Walker, Sydney, New South Wales, December 18, 1883, two
pages. Rhodes House Library; photograph courtesy Pacific and Asian History, Research School of Pacific and Asian Studies, Australian National University, Canberra.

big chair on deck, and then I wrapped myself in a 'possum rug and did not move all day, just letting the sea wash over me.

There were only nine of us went down, and we mostly knew each other so we had a fine time of it. There was Mr Thompson, Howard and myself a clergyman whose name was Mr Hay (you would have thought that he would rather have put a damper on the party, but he was a fine fellow, and never as much as put on a white tie or black coat all the time he was away, and could play a game of cards with anyone, and yet on a Sunday he could preach a splendid sermon).

Then there was Mr Syme and his son (He is brother of the editor of one of the papers here, so Mr Thompson, took them so that he could write an account of the trip &ct, I see by this mornings paper that he is bringing it out in the weekly paper, in numbers, the first lot out to day, so I will be able to send them to you, and you will be able to form your own idea of Fiji, and I should not wonder if he does not also publish a book about it, and if so I will send you a copy).

Next on the list was "Dr Dick," (doctor of a lunatic asylum here, a very nice fellow, and we found him very useful as we had a number of small accidents). Then there was a young fellow named "Jackson" from Sandhurst, and another named "Warburton" whose father was killed and eat by the natives of Fiji a few years ago. This comprised the whole lot of us and a very nice party we were, the only drawback were the two "Syuvés" who were such dirty beasts and, used to stuff themselves like pigs, until they could eat no more.

I had not a cabin myself as there are only two in the saloon (4 in each), but they were in Howards cabin, and they were rather too much for him, so he used to go in the captain's to dress himself, and slept with me in the saloon.

It was rather strange that not a soul on board from the captain downwards had ever been to Fiji before. We did not see many sights going down, passing a few islands (but unfortunately generally through the night). We saw a few seals and shot one or two albatrosses &ct.

Before we were a couple of days out, we found that the captain (he brought the steamer out from home) was not what he ought to be; he said that he was a teetotler, but it turned out that he was nothing of the sort, and that he was rather too fond of his liquor (he had a private supply in his cabin, and used to drink on the sly, but even now he will swear that drink never touched his lips all the voyage).

One night (or rather morning for it was about 2 o-clock) he nearly ran us on to a small island; everyone had turned in except Mr Thompson and myself (for I was always up if there was any land to pan, never mind what time it was) so we gave a hand in taking down the sails, and I got to the wheel, and we managed to keep clear of the island. Ever after that Mr Thompson (who, before would not believe that the captain drank although I told him) always kept his eye on him and told the chief mate to do the same. If Mr Thompson had not been on board I do not think that I should now be writing this letter to you.

We arrived off "Suva" on the Monday evening (11 days from Melbourne) but as it was dark, and being a very nasty place to enter, and amount of reefs about, we stayed outside till morning. I enjoyed myself that night immensely, the water being smooth (we had had it rough all the way from Melbourne) and the engines being stopped, everything so nice and quiet. I had been fishing over the stern of the ship with a small line, when all at once I had it carried away all together, so I guessed that there were some sharks about. I got a rope and fixed up a shark line, and in about five minutes I had a fine big shark hooked on. It took about a dozen of us to haul him up, and when we did get him on deck, he wanted to be master there, for he upset four or five of them with his tail, before they could clear out of the way. One of the sailors at last managed to cut off his tail (they say that this is the only way to kill them). He then cut him open and took out his heart, and cut off his head, and even then he was alive, his tail being put into his mouth he bit it in two.

Well! we were to have gone into "Suva" at daylight, so I turned in at two, and had an hours sleep, and then up again at three. When I got on deck I found that I was the only one up, and that they were just starting, although it was not daylight, so I went on the bridge and there I found the captain tight, and I could see that the ship was going on to the reefs, so I quietly went down, and got Mr Thompson up, and he got the chief mate up, and by that time it was getting daylight, so we got in all right.

The second mate was telling me that the captain would have run us ashore, if he himself had not gone to the wheel and altered the course of the ship.

Of course we were in before anyone was up, so we gave them a shot or two with the cannon which we had on board and which, soon had them all out, I think that it must nearly have frightened the life out of some of the niggers there, for a ship very seldom indeed calls there, but they soon came out to see what was the matter.

"Suva" is a splendid place, it nearly all belongs to Mr Thompson who has a store and an hotel there. These are the only buildings the rest being only huts. There are only about twenty white people here, and I should think that they have a very slow time of it altogether, there being of course nothing to do at all. The natives soon began to come off in there canoes, and before long the ship was swarming with them. They are a fine strong clan of men, but most fearfully lazy, and as they live on nothing but fish and fruit, it is as much as you can do to get them to work at all. We had some good fun with them, throwing money into the water, and letting them dive for it. If you throw a threepenny bit as far as ever you can, they will swim to the place where it dropped in the water, and then dive down, and are sure to get it before it, gets to the bottom. The women and men wear no clothing but a piece of rag round their middle (sometimes not even that much) and the children nothing at all.

After breakfast we went ashore in the boats. It was a peculiar sensation getting on land after all the rough weather we had had, and it took us all our time to walk straight, our legs being quite drunk. It was a little queer at first having a whole crowd of niggers round you, but after a little time you don't notice them at all, and get quite used to them.

We first of all went through the store, and then patronised the hotel (the only liquor they had was whisky and brandy) I think that we must have made the landlord more busy, then he had ever been since the hotel started.

Afterwards we went up to a Mr Joske's (whose brother in Melbourne is a great chum of Mr Thompson's). We there had a good blow out of fruit, and then some of us walked to the native village (which was about a mile and a half off). Here we had some great fun, such a row you never heard before (for I suppose that they do not see a white man, except those that live there from one years end to the other).

They had a good many curiosities to sell (clubs, spears, shells, bows & arrows &ct) We bought them all up, although I myself, only bought a few, as I thought that I would get better elsewhere (for which I was afterwards sorry). You can buy them very cheap, for instance clubs, beautifully carved and having the extra curiosity of having killed men, you can buy for a shilling or two, or a piece of tobacco.

The natives have nothing to sleep on but a mat, and a piece of wood for a pillow. It is very seldom that they do any work, for they live on fruit and fish, of which there is any amount. They will even only catch enough fish for themselves and will not catch any to sell. They do not catch their fish with lines, but go along the beach with spears, and directly they see a fish, they throw the spear at it and very seldom miss.

The following day we got up an excursion to go up the "Rewa" river. We hired a small sailing boat (as our ship boats would not go through the shallow places), and after taking in provisions and a cask of beer, we started about midday. We had some pretty good fun going up the river, and did ample justice to the provisions and beer. We arrived at "Rewa" about seven o-clock seeing nothing, particular, but the splendid scenery, and a few river snakes, and birds.

At "Rewa" we saw the greatest sight that was to be seen, namely a meeting of all the native chiefs and their tribes (this meeting only takes place either only once a year, or once every ten years, I forget which). They starve themselves for sometime before, so that they can bring as much food as possible to the feast (for it is nothing else). We were told that some of them had been almost starved to death, for although there was any amount of food about, yet the chiefs would not let them touch it, so that they might keep it, to take with them.

We arrived just in time to see one of the tribes dancing a "meca meca" or native dance. They all dress themselves out with beads and shells, painting themselves, till as they think, they are tremendous swells. The dancing was very well worth seeing, keeping such good time, they are brought up to it from children, so as to make themselves perfect, and so that they can beat other tribes as they are awfully jealous.

After the dance they all went to get their supply of food, which is served out to each tribe. They are all gathered together and then each lot receives their share. I forget how many pigs they had killed and were distributing the day we saw them, but I know that there were some good piles of them. They were all put in heaps according to their sizes, so many small ones, and so on till they came to the big ones. They are baked whole, and filled with stones (what for I don't know). The turtles were divided in the same way, they cook them alive, just putting them on the top of the fire, and eat nearly raw, they were very anxious that we should have some, but "not me." They have a pudding of their own manufacturing, I think that it is made chiefly of sugar I did not taste it but some of them did.

We saw them all feasting as we were going back, they all sit round in a ring, one man in the middle, with a knife, he cuts it up all in the dust and dirt, and the others eat it with their fingers, it was good fun seeing them cutting up a large pig, he does warm to his work.

I forgot to say that we were introduced to the King of the "Fiji islands" "King Cakobau." Every one has to kneel to him even the Governor, I did not care about doing it, as it was not a very nice thing to have to kneel to a nigger, however I thought that it was rather better to go down on one knee than to take the chance of getting a crack on the head.

He is an awful villain, and a few years ago, used to live on nothing but human flesh, even when a lad, they say, that if he was playing with a friend, he would think nothing of hitting him over the head and eating him.

We saw his canoe which is a tremendous thing, it was launched over the bodies of live men, two or three hundred being killed for the occasion. Nearly all the white people here, have seen them eating human flesh. Most of the chiefs now have big schooners of their own, and are very well off. I forget how many thousands the King is allowed by government.

After we had walked about a bit, we went to have a look at the hotel, where we were going to put up for the night. We found that they had nothing to eat in the house, so we had to fall back on our own provisions. After feeding we went over again to see the meeting, and hung about there till nearly one oclock in the morning.

It was intended that we should all have gone further up the river the next day, to see two sugar mills, which had lately been started, but the governor arriving at "Rewa" that evening and hearing of course that we were there, sent across to say that he would like to see Mr Thompson the next day.

However Howard and I and Warburton thought we might make a fine trip of it if we went by ourselves, so we told Mr Thompson, and got his gun from him, and without saying a word to anyone, took the owner of the boat, and three niggers, and started at three oclock in the morning. First of all I should tell you that the night before when we got to the hotel, we found that there was no where for us to sleep. He was putting up a new hotel, which had got half the floor down, no doors or windows in, and not an article of furniture of any description, and here we slept on the bare floor (for which he had the cheek to charge us 4 shillings ahead), or rather I did not sleep for as it was 2 o-clock I only lay down for a hour.

After we had got a little way up the river we had a bathe, and took the risk of sharks (for the water is thick with them). We then started eating (for you may be sure we took the provisions and beer with us), and we found that before nine oclock we had gone through breakfast, Lunch, dinner, tea, and supper, so we had to start afresh. I got some duck shooting, killing a good many, although we only managed to get a few of them; I made the niggers jump overboard and swim for them. We called at a small store to buy a few pineapples, but the man would not let us pay for them sending seven or eight dozen, to the boat for us, some of which we brought to Melbourne with us. Howard afterwards bought a whole lot of curiosities from them.

We arrived at the sugar mills at about eleven o-clock and after going through them, and taking a few sticks of sugar cane away with us, started back about one. Now, came the worst part of the trip, for we had the wind and tide against us.

We had promised to be back at "Rewa" by four o-clock, so that we might start back early for "Suva." Well! we were creeping along very slowly, bathing and shooting every now and then till we saw a big pig fall in the water and, snapped up by a shark; so I said no more bathing for this child. We did not get to "Rewa" until nine o-clock, and to shew you how hot it was, we managed to drink 24 bottles of beer between the three of us. We started back to "Suva" about half past nine, and after one or two narrow shaves for upsetting (for the boat was rather small for us 13), we arrived alongside the steamer about two o-clock, and I can tell you that I was glad for it was rather too much of a good thing to sit in that small boat for 23 hours.

We left "Suva" for "Laveuka" the same day, I slept the whole way, and although I was sleeping near the canon, it failed to wake me when it was fired off. "Laveuka" is only about 6 hours steaming from "Suva," it is built at the foot of a mountain, so that you get the sun blazing on you and not the slightest breeze. We soon had the ship crowded with people, coming off from shore, but unlike "Suva" as they were all whites and no blacks. There are a good few stores here, and even too chemists shops, and a good many boatmen for such a little place, they must have made nearly a fortune from us, rowing us to and from the ship. The natives here are a little more decent, the women wearing a covering over the shoulders, while one or two men I saw "sporting" hats.

The following day was Sunday, and the clergyman was ashore preaching. Some went to church, and most *not*. I stayed on board all day fishing for sharks but whether they would not bite on a Sunday, or not I don't know, but I could not get them to look at the hook, although directly anything was thrown over they, soon had it. The water was beautifully clear, and you could see thousands of small fish and shark's.

The following day we all received invitations to go to the governors, and I was the only one who refused, and I had by far the best of it, as they had all to turn out in black coats, which must nearly have killed them with heat.

We left "Laveuka" the next morning (Christmas morning) for "Suva," so that we were both at "Laveuka" and "Suva" on Christmas day. Most of them went ashore to Mr Joske's for their Christmas dinner, but I and Howard and one or two others staid on board, there was nothing extra happened, and everything passed off very quietly.

One of the chiefs was to have brought me a lot of curiosities to buy, but I found that he had had a row with another chief and that they were both in the lock-up, so that I came away with very few curiosities. I intended to have sent them home to you, but those that I have now, are hardly worth sending. I forget how long we staid in "Suva" this time, only a day or two I think.

Just as we got in, a labour vessel came in from the "Solomon islands" with three or four hundred niggers on board. They had nothing at all to eat on board, and had got disease amongst them, and were in a horrible state. In one place they had had a row for taking some cocoa-nuts, the chief mate was killed, and three or four of the seamen wounded, and one poor fellow had his hand taken off by a shark. They had been six months on the voyage. When we went on board every-one was drunk, and the poor black fellows, starving.

There were a splendid lot of curiosities on board, but they were too drunk to bargain with, however Mr Thompson bought a whole lot of parrots from them, and carried them safely to Melbourne with only the loss of two, one got away, and the other one drowned.

After we left "Suva" we went to "Maro," bringing with us Mr Thompsons brother in law, who manages their store, and a Mr Pooley, and three second class passengers, all of them coming on to Melbourne. At "Maro" Mr Thompson has a sugar plantation; but as it was six or seven miles up the river, only one or two of them went up, whilst most of us stayed on board. We only saw two natives (as the village was a long way off) who came off in their canoe, with a couple of kittens to sell, and because we would not buy them they threw them in the water, we managed to save one of them, and brought it with us to Melbourne.

I proposed that we should take one of the ships boats and go on shore, so away we went, and had not gone above half a mile before the plug came out of the boat and began to fill, frightening the life out of some of them, I however put my finger in the hole and managed to stop the water a little till they found the plug again, after all we had to turn back to the ship as we could not find a landing place. After we had put them on board, Howard and I took the boat and guns, and tried the other shore where we landed all right, and managed to shoot a lot of birds and fish.

We left "Fiji" for "Melbourne" the same evening and spent New Years day at sea, we had a little more excitement than on Christmas day as they were mostly Scotchmen on board, but beyond an awful row at twelve oclock, and a little extra whisky, nothing much happened, except indeed, that our dinner was spoiled through the cook getting drunk, and having a fight.

They were expecting to get in on Monday the 7th but on the Saturday it became fearfully rough with a head sea, and wind. Saturday night I did not get a wink of sleep, and was up all night, holding on by the "skin of my teeth." On Sunday morning it increased, and I wonder that some of us were *not killed,* for the things were flying about in all directions. One fellow I quite thought was killed, he had the ships-library, and five portmanteaus on the top of him at once. I had a portmanteau fall on my shoulder, but it did not do much damage. One night I was lifted from the saloon seats where I was sleeping, right on to the table and there I lay for a few moments, not knowing whether I was dead or alive.

The "hawser" go[t] washed overboard by the sea, and got entangled round the screw, as luck would have it, one of the "fan's" caught it and cut it in two else nothing would have saved [us] for it would have pulled up all the machinery. As it was there must have been 50 or 60£ [load] and more than half of it was lost.

The chief mate went over the side of the ship to put a rope round it to haul it up, and found that he could not get back again and one of the seamen had to go over to get him.

The next misfortune was the wheel to be carried away, but there were luckily two places to steer from so we had the other place, although they had packed cases of pine-apples all round it after that the governor of the engine broke, and so we found it was no use to try to get along with such a sea and head wind, and as we had only a day and a halfs coal on board (we were less than 24 hours steam from Melbourne if it had been smooth) we were frightened, that they would not last so we turned back to go into Sydney.

I was rather glad myself, as I have always had a longing to see "Sydney." By this time I was regularly dead beat from want of sleep, and as one of the engineers offered me his "bunk" while he was on duty, I went and lay down and had the best sleep for four hours that I had from the time I left Melbourne. He knocked me up at 12 oclock, and found that we could see Sydney lights in the distance, and saw the pilot steamer coming out for us, I was thankful to get inside the heads into smooth water, for the last day or two I had been wet through, by a big sea that washed over me and I was obliged to keep my clothes on as I had no change.

We anchored in Sydney at daylight on the 7th (my birthday, which I spent ashore). We went on shore after breakfast, and Howard and I went paying calls all morning, and in the afternoon, took a carriage, and drove out to the gardens and round the harbour. Sydney is the prettiest place I have ever been in, and I like it far better than Melbourne.

There are some splendid buildings, having got very good stone there. I went to see the pantomime in the evening which was the only thing that I was dissapointed with in Sydney.

Howard and Warburton had made up their minds to stay in Sydney for a day or two and go overland to Melbourne. So we left them, and at daylight we left for Melbourne. I saw a number of people I knew in Sydney, including Mr Drysdale.

The passage from Sydney to Melbourne was so calm that there was not a ripple on the water, and we had a splendid time of it. Nothing happened very much on the way, I shot a porpoise with a revolver. We arrived off the Heads about seven oclock, on Friday evening.

We drank Mr Thompsons health &ct going down the bay and arrived at Williamstown at about ten oclock, I left the ship here (as I was expecting Howard would be home about that time and I was trying to get home before him) and took a boat across to Sandridge where I got a cab and drove home, and found a telegram from Howard saying that he would not be home till the following day.

Altogether we had a splendid trip of it, and I enjoyed myself immensely.

I found my letters waiting for me here, and was glad to find so many for me.

I found one from Mr Sandiford, asking me to go and spend Christmas with him, and get some shooting, which I was sorry to have to decline as he has now asked me four or five times. Howard is next going to Adelaide, but I do not think he will leave till next week or the week afterwards. I forgot to tell you that the two "Chamberlaines" of Birmingham were down in "Fiji," but they unfortunately left "Laveuka" the day we arrived; we heard that they had been buying a tremendous lot of curiosities. Howard after-wards met them at Sydney. I have not been to Mr Thompsons since we arrived, I intended to have gone on Sunday but it looked like rain, so I had to put it off.

The Pantomimes are all hard at it still, but they [are] not quite up to the mark. We have the Circus here as well, with a lot of addi-tions to it. The "Lusitania" arrived this morning (January 22) but Mr Reece has not been up yet. I expect that he will go on to New Zealand to-morrow, as there is a boat leaving.

Work, seemed a little strange at first, after five weeks idleness, but now I have got into it all right. I have asked Mr Rigg for a move from where I am now, as I have been here for 18 months now, I shall ask him again and if he does not move me, I shall [feel] in-clined to move out altogether myself.

I am very much obliged to you for the chain, I did not think that I should get any presents at all. Sallie says in her letter that she and Willie have sent me out a locket with Mr Reece, so I suppose that I shall get them all tomorrow. Well! I think that I have written a long enough letter this mail, so the others can hardly expect to get any till next, as this is a family letter with love to all[.]

Believe me

Your loving son

<u>VL Walker</u>

January 23*rd* "Reece" has just been in, and brought my parcel, I like the chain very much indeed. He is going on to New Zealand to day, so excepting the few minutes he was here, I shall not see anything of him.

Commentary

When Walker wrote the preceding letter he was twenty-one years old and had been in Australia for three years. He was working for McLean, Bros., and Rigg, Importers and General Ironmongers, whose specialties, accord-ing to an advertisement of the time, included Nobel's Genuine Dynamite, "Hardware Novelties," and "Squatting Supplies." Times were prosperous enough for a holiday of sorts; this holiday may have been provided for by William Kerr Thomson, a family friend who owned a good deal of land in New Zealand and Fiji as well as in Victoria; his activities seemed to have

paved the way for the later trading activities in the Pacific of Walker's somewhat domineering elder brother, Howard. For these men, recreation seems
mainly to have meant shooting. At various points on the journey, seals,
ducks, "one or two albatrosses," other birds, and fish are shot—though not
for eating; sharks too are caught and cut up. This is unremarkable entertain-
ment. Between Sydney and Melbourne on the way back, "nothing happened
very much on the way, I shot a porpoise with a revolver." It is difficult,
for me at least, to avoid considering this a violent life. That assessment, of
course, depends on certain values of the present; just as those who ethno-
centrically denigrated Melanesian headhunters ignored the ritual meanings
of that kind of killing—its value in a system of ancestor worship and pro-
pitiation—my, or our, abhorrence of Walker's way of destroying life passes
over its meaning and interest for men of his time. They certainly had their
culture, which is not the same as mine; but that fact does not make it easier
to understand this careless sport. Regarding it as a kind of ritual does not
help; some rituals are enacted through dull habit rather than vital energy.

Walker often presents himself, not as an actor, but as a person directed by
others: he had not intended to participate in the trip, but at the last minute
"Mr Thompson said [he] had better come." This passivity and carelessness
make him almost an object to which things happen; during the bad weather
on the voyage out he sits on deck all day, without moving, "just letting the
sea wash over me." Walker's apparent lack of will to shape either his own
course or surrounding affairs is manifest again in the way that the letter describes and situates Fiji. What it does is most striking if we consider another
account of the same trip, an account that Walker refers to. The Symes mentioned near the beginning are members of the famous Melbourne family
that owned the leading daily newspaper, the *Age,* in which a five-part account of the trip appeared:

> The result of a recent trip to Fiji has been to impress me most favor-
> ably in regard to the industrial capabilities of the country, and its
> future commercial prosperity . . . I consider it most desirable that the
> people of Victoria should get acquainted with the youngest of our colo-
> nies, since a better acquaintance might not only induce them to take
> a deeper interest in its affairs than they appear to take at present, but
> might also be the means of enabling them to see their way to the in-
> vestment of capital, and to the bestowal of some of their characteristic
> energy in the development of its resources. ("Papalan-hi" 1878: 7)

35

The writer proceeded to still more optimistic claims—that Fiji could be for Australia what the West Indies had been to Europe—and came back to such questions at many points in his report. But the islands were attractive to the tourist as well as the investor or settler:

> During the greater part of the voyage you sail over placid, summer seas, sighting innumerable islands, which raise their brown and purple peaks above the sunlit waves. You see some features of nature peculiarly characteristic of that quarter of the world, and to be met with nowhere else, as, for instance, the coral reefs which form; beautiful but dangerous circles round each of the islands, and the cocoa-nut palm trees which supply the natives with food and drink and almost all they need. You see the way in which the natives live, blending in their character a good deal of the barbarism out of which they are just emerging, and a little of the Christian civilisation which has been placed within their reach. You see new aspects of nature, and new phases of life. (Ibid.)

No mention here of the hazards and discomfort of the trip—a drunken captain, reefs, and storms—but what is striking about the newspaper account are not its trite fabrications of a sanitized, pleasant tour, but the article's larger coherence. It is of course a typically dull piece of colonial journalism, and it is hard to distinguish from many other accounts of Fiji of the period, which were extremely repetitive on the subject of the islands' resources and prospects, but the text possesses a certain completeness and composure, which Walker's franker and fragmentary narrative lacks. The journalist positions Fiji on the periphery of an expanding frontier; people are about to know the place better, to visit in greater numbers, to expand settlement and increase production. The islands present themselves both as novel prospects and novel sights; just as the eye is excited and inspired by the scenery and the natives, energy is stimulated by the scope for investment and development. This vision is informed both by precise geographical knowledge (the total area is "nearly equal to that of Wales") and ethnological understanding: land tenure and traditional government through chieftainship can be described. Fijians are at once objects of anthropological speculation—could their cannibal natures really be altered by Christianity? —and "grotesque" characters who provide amusement and spectacle:

> They were . . . not repulsive. They were rather an appropriate adjunct of the scene. How could we have believed that we were in Fiji at all, unless we had seen just such grotesque fellows as these we saw cluster-

ing on the deck, or squatting on the bows of their canoes, or swimming about in the water. (Ibid.)

Fiji, then, is not somewhere that one can simply be; one needs to be persuaded that one is in such an exotic place, and belief can be confirmed by a kind of measurement: the natives are as grotesque as one expects.

Walker appears uninterested in the larger narrative that the *Age* writer imagines. Of course, he comes out with some of the standard observations: the Fijians are utterly idle, though their fastidiousness in preparing for their dances attests to their jealousy and vanity; and he, like so many others, was at least mildly titillated by the prospect of owning a cannibal's club. (The interest, incidentally, made the manufacturing of "cannibal" weapons something of an export industry even as early as the 1870s; they were made mainly by pacific and Christian Fijians unlikely to have ever killed anyone.) But just as Walker is not interested in the specific natures of Fijians—they and the Solomon Islander indentured laborers alike are simply "niggers"— neither is he concerned with the future of Fiji, which is such a weighty issue for Syme's ponderous report. Walker refrains from representing the islands and the journey in terms of an aesthetic and inquisitive possessiveness that would accompany economic appropriation; his "ethnological" observations are marked by a carelessness that is almost refreshing after the false and tedious precision that characterizes much colonial anthropological and travel writing. So the feast witnessed at Rewa took place "either only once a year, or every ten years, I forget which."

July 19*th* 1880
65 Pitt S*t*

My dear mother

I am beginning to think that I must have dropped out of the memory of all at home, for I have not heard from any one (except one letter from you) since I have been in Sydney. That letter was dated March 25th, so that I have had no news from home for four months, I thought at first that my letters must have gone to Melbourne, so I wrote to make enquiries and found that there were none there for me. There was a letter from you to Howard arrived last mail and I have sent it on to him.

I sent you a newspaper by the "San Francisco" mail last week with an account of the capture of the "Kelly gang," who have managed to elude the police for the last two years, there was tremendous excitement here while the fight was going on, hundreds of people outside the newspaper offices, watching for the telegrams as they came in, with the accounts of the fight, as it was proceeding. In Melbourne I believe the excitement was still worse, and people even shut their shops, so that all could go and watch the telegrams as they came in. "Ned Kelly" who was captured alive has not yet recovered sufficiently to appear at his trial, but they expect that he will be well enough this week.

Howard has been away in Adelaide and Melbourne for the last three weeks, so that I have been left by myself here, and have found plenty to do, I expect him back again, in four or five days. He went overland to Melbourne, and happened to be passing "Glenrowan" railway station, while the fight with the "Kelly's" was going on, and stayed there to watch it, so I expect full account of it on his return here.

I feel very dull in Sydney after Melbourne, and as yet have made very few friends here, and if it was not for the harbor I don't know what I should do on Saturdays and Sundays.

I wonder if you are still thinking of coming out here for a trip. I have been waiting anxiously to hear from you every mail, if you are still thinking of coming, but I am always dissappointed and do not receive any letters at all.

Melbourne, I expect is very lively now preparing for the Exhibition and I hope that business may take me over there, so that I may get a chance of seeing it, as I only just saw the finish of the "Sydney" one, I am sending our exhibit over to-morrow, but it will have to wait some time there before it will be opened.

I thought that Melbourne was bad enough for news, but I find that Sydney is worse, for I have no news at all, to tell you, so must conclude, with love to all

Your loving son
V Lee Walker

I enclose a photograph I had taken, just before leaving Melbourne, I did not intend sending any home, as I have never had a photograph (I make a mistake I had *one*, Harry's) sent me since I left Bromley House.

December 21st 1880
65 Pitt S^t

Dear mother

I suppose that Howard, in his letters has told you why I have not been able to write to you for the last mail or two.

At the last minute Mr Thomson talked me into going another trip to "Fiji" with him, and I have not regretted accepting his offer for I could not have enjoyed any trip more.

I with Howard was down on board the steamer to say good by to them before they left (they were leaving at daylight) and it was about one oclock in the morning when I said that I would go, so I just went home put my things with my portmanteau, came back again and turned into the first empty bunk I came to, & by daylight we were steaming down the harbour. It was the Prince of Wales birthday (Nov 9th) when we left Sydney & you could not have got a more miserable day, for it was raining hard & the sea was fearful rough, as there was a gale of wind blowing. Things went very quiet for the first two or three days, as everyone was sea-sick, myself included (although I thought that I was never going to be sea-sick again). There were between 20 & 30 of us on board most of them new-chums, amongst them "Cartland" (Howards friend from Birmingham). "Howard" of Bedford (son of the great Implement makers) & "Ward" of Sheffield (son of Ward of Ward & Payne the sheep-shear makers). Altogether their was a decent lot (I forgot to mention that we had a parson, as Mr Thomson never travels with out a parson on board)

We passed "Lord Howes Island" & "Norfolk Island," but it was too rough to land at either places, so we had to put off our visit till the return trip from "Fiji."

We arrived at "Suva" on Friday November 19th, having had bad weather all the way down.

I should have told you the object of Mr Thomsons trip to Fiji. The whole of "Suva" belongs to Mr Thomson, & "Leveuka" the present capital, not being a large enough place Mr Thomson says to the government I will *give* you three fifths of "Suva," if you will promise me to make that place the capital. The Government accepted his offer & November 22nd was the first Land sale day.

Not arriving till the Friday & the land-Sales being on the Monday we did not think that it would be worth while leaving "Suva" so we sent the steamer on to "Leveuka" & we put up at the Hotel on shore. On the Monday, of course, there was great excitment about the sales, as the "Leveuka" people were going to do all they could to spoil it, for the moving of the capital meant the ruin of a lot of them who had property at "Leveuka." However the sale went off better than anyone expected and the "Leveuka" people had to buy themselves. It was only Government land that was sold, but Mr Thomson sold a lot of his afterwards privately, & got nearly double the price of the government lands.

The next day we all went up the "Rewa" river in a small steamer, & we were away for two days, but the pleasure of this trip was spoilt by all of us getting wet through to the skin the first day, & none of us having a change. You never saw such dirty miserable creatures as we looked when we returned to "Suva"

When we arrived at "Suva," we found that the steamer had returned and was waiting for us, so at 3PM that day (25th) we left for "Leveuka" where we arrived at ten oclock the same night. At 3PM the next day we left "Leveuka" for "Mango," where we arrived at 8 oclock the next morning. "Mango" Island belongs to four brothers named "Ryder," and is a perfect "Paradise," it is no use trying to describe it, because it would be impossible. The four brothers take alternate years of work, and pleasure, two of them are on the island for twelve months, whilst the other two travel round the world for pleasure, then at the end of every twelve months they change places. They have a house at each end of the Island about 4 miles apart, & have a telephone at work between the two of them. They employ about 6 white people & between 300 & 400 natives & grow cheifly cotton, sugar, coffee & maize & cocoa-nuts for copra. Thousands of tons of fruit of every description you can name, lying rotting on the ground, as they can't eat it and can't export it. It is impossible to descibe what the island is like, but I have never

41

seen such a beatuiful place *anywhere* talk about flowers & scenery. Ah well! it is no use talking about them for no one could believe it unless they saw it. It was well worth the travelling of the 2000 miles to see that Island alone. We were all very sorry when evening came and we had to leave it & go on the "Taviwui," which place we reached the next morning at daylight, but this being a very religeous Island (and it being Sunday 28th.) as there are a great number of missionary's here, every thing was very quiet, and I fancy we were all thinking of "Mango Island," which took all the shine out of this Island. However we spent a very pleasant day, and left again in the evening for "Leveuka" arriving there the next morning Monday 29th at 9AM. Here we stayed two days as we had to take in cargo. We gave the "Leveuka" people a big lunch "on board," & they gave us a big dinner on shore and altogether we spent a very pleasant two days. We had a photograph taken of the lot of us in a group, and I well send you one of them as soon as they arrive. (They are to come up by the next steamer which is daily expected). From "Leveuka" we went back to "Suva," and from "Suva" on December 2nd at 3PM we started back for Sydney.

On the 6th we arrived at "Norfolk Island," and here also we spent a day. It is as I daresay you know an old Convict settlement and the ruins of the prison &ct are still there. We walked across the island (between 3 & 4 miles) through an avenue of Norfold Island Pines, and on the other side met Bishop "Selwyn," and fifteen or sixteen clergimen who had come from Auckland to consecrate a church. We went inside the church, which was as pretty a one as ever I went into, the floor being beautifully laid with marble. The church was put up in memory of Bishop Patterson who was murdered by the natives amongst the Islands (Norfold Isld is always the Bishops head quarters) & which I am afraid will be the end of "Bishop Selwyn" for there have been a great number of murders lately. Before we left I had some good fishing. I was the only one on board who knew anything about deep-sea fishing, and having my own tackle with me I got on first rate, whilst the others could not understand why they could not catch any. I supplied the ship with fish for three days.

We left Norfolk Island the same evening and arrived at "Lord Howes" Island on December 8th 8PM, but it being dark, we were not able to land. However we had some good sport on board.

About ten oclock I put the shark lure overboard and almost before the bait touched the water we had a shark hooked and amongst any amount of yelling and howling (not the shark) we got him on board. Well! to make a long story short, for two hours we hauled in sharks as fast as ever we could, and at that time our arms ached so, that we had to leave off as fast as we caught them the sailors chopped off their tails (the only way to kill them) & through them overboard, and the others seeing their wounded would attack and eat them. We counted the tails, and found 25 so it was not a bad nights work (it would have been more fun in the daylight, as it was very dangerous at night as, they were plenty big enough to bite ones legs off, luckily there were no accidents.

In the morning the wind began to blow and a boat came off and told us not to attempt to land as it was too rough. This was a fearful dissappointment to us as we had all intend[ed] to have had some fine shooting, as there were any amount of wild pigs & goats on the Island.

There are only 48 people on the Island, and no ship ever calls there, at least they think themselves very lucky if they here twice a year from the other world. If that is but being buried alive, I dont know what is; They do not have to work at all, as everything grows so luxuriantly. We had another dissappointmeant, as we intended to have all got a supply of fruit to take to our friends in Sydney. We did not get any from Fiji (at *least I* only got a bunch of "bananas" & a few pineapples) as they said "what's the good of carrying it when you can get any amount at "Lord Howes Island," which is only two days steam from Sydney." Well we had to go without our fruit, and at 8AM we started for "Sydney." The captains words were soon verefied, and we were very soon in a gale which lasted for 24 hours. We arrived in Sydney on Saturday Dec-11th 9AM after the pleasantest trips I ever spent & doubly so as it is a trip that none of us will have the chance of ever going again.

Mr Thomson was the only one who had bad news waiting for him "his fathers death in Glasgow" You must know that we were like out of the world for five weeks, as there is no telegraph & we could here of nothing from the time we left till the time we returned & when they told me that "Hanlou" had beaten "Trickett" I couldn't believe it, however I found that it was true.

I found pleanty of work when I came back, and have been busy ever since, espescially as Howard has gone to Melbourne I expect him back in a few days when he is going to "New Caledonia" & will be away for a month.

I have had a very bad throat ever since I came back from "Fiji" & for two or three days I was frightened about it as I could not swallow at all, it is better now, but I cannot get it quite well, although I have been taking care of myself. We went round the harbour in a steam launch & got caught in a "scuall" & got wet through so I think that I must have caught cold.

I have missed the mail for wishing you a merry Christmas but I hope that you will have had one, and will have a very Happy New Year

Your loving son

V Lee Walker

September 19th/81
102 Clarence S^t
Sydney

Dear Cyril

I found your short letter waiting for me here, on my return from New Zealand, and I have been so busy that I have not had time to answer it before.

I had a long trip through New Zealand, four months of it, and at the very worst time of the year, nothing but rain, snow, frost and wind, I was pretty glad to get back to warm weather again, for I can't stand cold after living in a hot climate for five years, "things ain't as they used to was." In doing New Zealand you have to go through a lot of coaching, & being stuck on the box of a coach for two days at a stretch (and some of them *are* days from half two in the morning till eleven at night), & raining and snowing is not what you may call travelling for pleasure, I had lots of accidents and adventures, but nothing very serious. The worst I think was being upset in a river, whilst crossing in a coach, the driver mistook the ford, and before we knew where we were, we were upset coach and all in five feet of water. We managed to save the horses and luggage, (the latter of course soaking), but we had to leave the coach in the river, & wait in our wet clothes for two hours for another coach, and did not reach our destination till eleven at night, without even a dry collar to put on.

I was wet through for nearly three weeks, and of course had to suffer in the shape of rheumatism. The next time I make a trip to New Zealand I hope that it will be in the summer months.

Thanks for your photo. I do not know if I sent you one of my last or not, but all my things are packed up in cases and goodness only knows, when I will have time to open them up but when I do I will send you one of mine.

Howard has gone down to "Noumea" in his new steamer "The

India," and will I expect be away for about a month, so that I have plenty of work to do while he is away, and don't care how soon he comes back.

Business has been very slack, but I think is looking up a little now. Well! this is mail day so you must excuse a long letter, and when I have a little spare time I will drop another line or two.

Your affec^{te} brother.

<u>V. Lee. Walker.</u>

Cyril W Walker Esqre
Wolverhampton

October 25th/82
163 Clarence S^t
Sydney. N.S.W.

Dear mother,

I find that I have not had a letter from home since last January, so I fancy it is about time I wrote a line and give you what little news I can.

I have not been out of Sydney since I last wrote to you, and I begin to feel in want of a change. I was going down to New Caledonia, for a trip in about a fortnights time but Howard is down there now, and unless he returns, next week, I shall not be able to get away for another six weeks.

Howard went down to New Caledonia last week, but I do not think that he will remain there for long. We were expecting Mr David Storer, out here this year, but we got a cablegram from him two days ago, and I do not think that he will come out now. Howard is talking of going home next March, but he has been talking of going home for so long that I shall not believe it, until he has really left, I wonder how long it will be before I am able to take a trip home, I have felt awfully home-sick the last year or two, and I fancy, get more so every day. I suppose that I would hardly find my way about Wolverhampton now. I should like to see you take a trip out here, the journey is nothing now, and it is well worth a trip to see the Colonies.

We have got awful swell offices here now, in fact, as nice as anyone in town, and have got plenty of store room.

I suppose you will have heard about out Exhibition being burnt down, it was a tremendous blaze, I could feel the heat, where I live, which is more than a mile away, by this Post I send you an illustrated paper, with a full account of the fire.

We had a big fire three doors from our office, a little time ago, which was a little too near to be pleasant considering we had about 2000 drums of oil in the place; we should have had a nice blaze.

I got a newspaper from Willie this mail, which is the only Wolverhampton news I have had this year. I notice that Mary Morton is married and the Mrs W.W.W. has given a basket of "Kidney beans," to the hospital.

I was very glad to hear from Howard, that Norman, had got such a good billet. I wonder if he has altered as much as Cyril, when I got Cyril's photograph, some time ago, I did not at first recognise him, he has grown such a swell, I enclose a rough photograph, I and some friends had taken, during a boating excursion, I am afraid that it will take you all your time to recognise me, although I do not think that I have altered much. Has anyone had any photographs taken lately, if so I wish you could manage to beg or steal some for me, after not seeing them for eight years. How the time does fly. I have forgotten my own age, the years pass so quickly, and taking no notice of my birthdays as they pass. Am I 25, or 26? I fancy that I must be somewhere about that.

Nov 7th I have been so busy that I have not had time to finish this letter before. Howard is still in New Caledonia, but I expect him back this day week. All last week I was so busy that I hardly knew what to do with myself, I was at the office every morning at 'past five, & until 10 & 11 at night, so that I had quite enough of it. Thank goodness, I have got pretty square with everything now.

Thursday the 9th (Prince of Wales Birthday) is a holiday for us, but unfortunately our steamer is going away, on that date so that I am afraid it will put a stop to my holiday. Well! it is mailday today and I am up to my neck in work, so I must bring my letter to a close. Hoping all at home are in good health,

Your lovin[g] son

V. Lee Walker.

January 8*th*/83
163 Clarence S*t*

My dear mother.

Your letter of November 2*nd*, was forwarded on to me to New Caledonia, where I have been for the last month, and you can imagine how glad I was to hear from you once more, for it is such a long time since I last received a letter from you. I was very pleased to receive your photograph, I could not have wished for a better Christmas box and only wish that I could get more of the others to send me their photographs; Sallie has sent me her children's photographs' the little girl is very like her, in fact they both are.

I left for Nouméa on December 1*st*, it is only a four days trip in the steamer, and we had a nice lot of passengers on board.

Of course I have met nearly all the Nouméa people in Sydney, and as I only made up my mind to go to Nouméa the night before the steamer left, I took them all by surprise. I stayed with some bachelor friends of mine, and never enjoyed a trip more. I will give the Nouméa people credit for knowing how to live; all their work is done in the early morning before breakfast. You get up at five, go to your office till ten o-clock, when you go home to breakfast, which takes till twelve or after, when you have your smoke a sleep for an hour, a bath, then back to the office till four or five oclock, then drive (every one has a trap of some sort) for an hour, and then go home to dinner, and to bed early. They know how to feed you, and take things very easy. The people there are very nice and I only wish I could have stayed for another month. I did not go very far inland as it was my first trip, and could not very well get away from Nouméa breakfast with one, dinner with another nearly every day, however I managed to get round the coast as far as our Chrome mine, and stayed there two days, I was greatly pleased with it.

My Christmas day I spent at sea, on the way back to Sydney it was a miserably rough day, and I don't think a soul on board enjoyed their Christmas dinner, everyone was sick from the captain down-wards, I did not eat a bite all day, in fact I never left the deck. We arrived in Sydney on boxing day, and as ill-luck would have it we ran aground when coming alongside the wharf, which kept us so long, that we lost that holiday as well. Of course I have been awfully busy since my return, and have got any amount of private letters to write, so much so that I have had to come back to the office this (Saturday) afternoon, and will be writing all day to-morrow. New Years day I was back at the office, and it is only to-day that I have got square with my work. On Monday the English mail goes out, and on Tuesday the New Caledonian mail comes in so that I shall have my hands full next week.

Howard was to have gone home in the "Ballarat," the steamer which takes this letter, but he now finds that he cannot get away till the next P & O boat, leaving here on the 26th, I make a mistake in saying that he was to have gone by the steamer which takes this letter, the steamer he was to have gone with, does not leave till the end of next week however you ought to see him three weeks or a month after you receive this; I only wish that I was going with him I do not think that he will remain away long, I expect him back in about six or eight months after he leaves.

We have had a very cool summer here as yet, in fact I feel it cold, after Nouméa, but we have had plenty of rain, so that the farmers cannot grumble.

I have written to "Chuckling" this afternoon, I think that there is a very good chance for her husband, but he would have to begin at the bottom of the ladder, to get Colonial experience, which means starting as a carpenter at £10/- per day, and I think I could safely promise him a billet at that.

Hoping, dear mother, that you are still keeping good health, and that you will have a happy year before you

Believe me
Your loving son
V. Lee Walker.

Howard goes home by the "Natal" leaving here February 3rd

September 3rd/83
Sydney. N.S.W.

My dear mother.

I have been so busy since Howard's return, that I have not had time to write to you before. I have to thank you very much for the £10/-/- which you sent me, you may be sure that it was very welcome. Howard was only here a week when he had to hurry off to New Caledonia on business; he took Louie with him. Louie seems to like Sydney she saw a great deal of it during the week she was here, & I had the pleasure of showing her round. I am sorry to say that Howard had bad news on his arrival here, as one of the largest houses in New Caledonia have suspended payment. However I fancy that it will turn out all right, and that we shall not lose anything. I am afraid that Howard will have some difficulty in getting a house to suit him here, as nice houses are awfully scarce just now, and rents are something frightful. Only part of his furniture has arrived, so that even if he got a house, he could not very well get into it, till the remainder arrived. We have had some excitement over the Irish informers, who came out. They were not allowed to land, and have been put on board a man-of-war down the harbour, from whence they will be sent back, home again.

George, who you will remember went home with Howard, has gone back to his old billet on board the "City of Melbourne," he has had some fine yarns to tell about his travels. I have chaffed him about going back to Mary's ship (I suppose that you have heard Howard speak about her, she is the stewardess). He seems to have been great friends with the girls at Bromley House, and I am sure that if he were here now, that he would send his love to them all. There is a steamer from New Caledonia due here to-day, and Howard may return by her, although I do not expect them till the end of the week, when there is a large steamer due.

I have hardly had time to have a talk with Howard since his return, but he seems to have enjoyed his trip, short as it was. I have met a friend of Norman's here, Walker, of "Walker's Whisky," and have had to show him around town he is staying here for a month.

Well! I do not think that I have any more news to tell you, so, hoping that you are keeping in good health, and with love to all at home.

Believe me, dear mother
Your loving son
V. Lee Walker

I was looking up this morn & find that it is now eight years since I left home I wonder how many years it will be till I see it once more?

Sydney N.S.W.
December 18*th*/83

My dear mother,

I was pleased to find a letter lying on my desk, from you when I came in to the office the other morning. I have no foreign note paper in the office, and this is the only sheet I can rake up, and it is not as clean as it might be.

Howard has at last got a house, strange to say it is in the same terrace where I am living, which will be handy. For a house in town, it is the best situation you could wish for, the front view is looking right down the harbour and from the back you look right up the Parramatta river, there is always a cool breeze, and very few mosquitoes. It is now being papered and painted & I do not suppose that they will get into it till the middle of January.

The only objection to it is the approach as you have to pass through the part of town where the chinamen live, and the smell of their cooking is not always the sweetest; omnibusses however pass the door every three minutes, so that you need never walk. We are getting into the warmer weather now, and we have had one or two very hot days.

Howard has had a lot of trouble lately, the last was the death of our agent in Nouméa (Mr Williams). He was a most particular friend of Howard's, and had splendid prospects before him. The poor fellow was getting on to his horse, when the horse shied, and threw him, on to his head. He was on[ly] 31 years of age and leaves a wife and three children, his wife only being confined about three days before the accident.

Howard, Louie, and myself are dining with a Mr. Nossitter on Christmas day, you may be sure that we shall not forget you at home. I am not going out of town for the holidays, and do not know what I shall do to pass away the time.

We are very busy in the office day as we are two hands short one being on the sick, & one away for a fortnights holiday Mr Rigg of McLean Bros & Rigg died last Sunday and is to be buried to-day, he has left a number of friends behind him, and will be greatly missed.

I fancy that I owe Cyril a letter, tell him that I will most likely answer it during the holidays, I am such an awful bad correspondent, and there is no news of any interest to those at home.

I am rather late in wishing you a Merry Christmas, but I trust that you will have a Happy & Prosperous New year. Hoping that all are well at home

Believe me, my dear mother
Your loving Son
<u>V. Lee Walker.</u>

Commentary

We reproduce only a few of Walker's letters from the years between 1878 and 1883. He wrote frequently and repetitively, acknowledging regular letters from his mother, expressing disappointment when they did not arrive, noting events in the social calendar such as pantomimes, and conveying the sense that his brother Howard was enjoying a social and commercial whirl, to which Lee was largely peripheral. Despite the apparent condition of prosperity, Lee often seems at a loose end, and evidently isolated. It is Howard who has the opportunity to visit home, Howard who owns the business, he who directs Lee to travel or not travel, to take a place or not in the boat, and he who is married or about to be married, and is making arrangements concerning houses, furniture, and wallpaper.

Up until 1883, the letters imply a genteel existence, a circuit of drives, of meals, and engagements; the main difficulty seems to be in getting a "nice house." Lee, however, mentions "bad news" in September 1883, and by December is reporting that "Howard has had a lot of trouble lately." We do not encounter many more references to drives in traps, and the social life seems to become less hectic. Even at this time Walker must thank his mother for a gift of £10; whether this was solicited because of some hardship is not clear, but there is a suggestion that the story, the plot of "Colonial experience" that Lee recommends for another correspondent's husband, is coming unstuck. The notion behind this is glimpsed in the reference to the "splendid prospects" of Williams, which were sadly extinguished by his accident. Society at home is crowded and restrictive; in the colonies, a working man must start from the bottom and work hard, but ultimately has better and brighter opportunities in their open spaces than in the metropolitan, industrial congestion of cities such as Wolverhampton. If this is so, he ought to be sending remittances rather than receiving them.

Walker says in a later letter that at Christmas his thoughts "naturally turn towards home," and his mention of photographs in January 1883 reminds us of how familial ties were reduced by time and distance to fragile threads of too-occasional correspondence, to mementos such as photographs, lockets, and chains. His niece and nephew, he finds, resemble their mother; his memory of her, by now, must be as indistinct as one of those sepia photographs that—if still preserved in the possession of some descendant alive now—would be faded and jumbled with others, and with other familial detritus, in a rarely opened desk drawer. But, of course, it is not the resemblance that is important; the statement is more a way of saying "I am still here." Walker enunciates, or feels obliged to enunciate, a continuing familial tie that seemed perhaps to be fraying: "it is such a long time"; "I . . . only wish I could get more of the others to send me their photographs."

This is a period of some security, initially even one of optimism; the life in Noumea appears to be attractive, and if residence in the Rocks is marred by the stink of Chinese food, it sounds as if the bus service was better then than it is now. But even in this period, there is a sense of lack and isolation; not leaving town for the holidays, Walker doesn't know what he'll do "to pass away the time." And if dinner with Mr. Nossiter and the death of Mr. Rigg suggest a degree of society, the presence of men who will be missed by many friends, there is also a hint of an absence of value: "there is no news of any interest to those at home."

July 29*th* 1884
Nouméa

My dear mother

If ever anyone ought to be ashamed of themselves, it is I, for I cannot remember when I last wrote to you, & although I might have excuses for not writing to other people, yet I should have no excuse in not writing to you.

Things here, have changed greatly, since I last wrote to you, but I suppose that you will have had full particulars from Howard and Louie.

I am very, very sorry to hear of Louie's return home, I have been away from Nouméa for a trip all round the Island, & only heard of her departure, on my return (a week or so, ago). I am afraid that she will not have a good opinion of me, & I daresay that there are lots of little things, which I might have done, to make her stay more pleasant, but having been out of decent society for so many years, I am afraid that I must have appeared a rather uncouth brute, however I meant well, even if I did not behave so.

As I said before, I have been for a trip round the coast, and although it was very rough work, I enjoyed myself thoroughly & only wish that I was going to start the same trip over again to-morrow, for I am miserable in Nouméa, as I have no friends & I see very little of Howard I have just a bedroom, & take my meals out, & hardly speak a word to anyone from the time I get up until I go to bed. I come home after dinner (as to-night) and write letters, or if I do not write letters, go to bed, as the offices open here, at seven oclock in the morning, so one has to get up early.

The trip I took was in our own schooner, a little bit of a boat with two beds in it, if you can call them beds, for I slept on the boards with just a blanket round me & went about without boots all the time as one has to walk through the water so much, that it is no use wearing boots, only when you have to walk two or three miles over coral, it is rather trying, but you soon get used to it. The greatest objection I had at first was the cock-roaches, although I got used to even them after a time. The ship was full of them, great big fellows two or three inches long, who used to crawl over your face whilst you were asleep, which was, (to say the least of it) anything but pleasant. We managed to run on a reef, & I never expected to see land again, as it was nasty weather at the time, however we were lucky enough to get off, with not much damage to the ship, but it took us two or three days to recover our spirits again. The captain is a very decent fellow (an Irishman), so it was a comfort to have someone to talk to after being with no-one but Frenchmen for some time. Dangerous as it is, travelling round the coast I would far sooner, be doing it, than having to live in Nouméa, for I never feel well in this beastly place, whereas I got as fat as a pig during my trip. I wonder when I will be able to take a trip home. I am afraid that it will be a long time yet, but I would like to have a look at you all again, for I was only a boy when I left and would see things in a very different light now, although I am afraid that I would never be able to stand the cold, for I complain of it here sometimes, & goodness knows, it is hot enough in this place I had a letter from Sallie a mail or so ago, but have not answered it as yet & I have an idea that I owe Nellie a letter, however I will try to write to them next mail, but letter writing is an awful job for me, for I am an awful bad hand at it.

Well! I think that it is time for me to go to bed, & will endeavour to write a little more regularly to you. With love to all

Believe me

Your loving Son

V. Lee Walker

Nouméa, New Caledonia
February 3*rd* 1885

My dear mother,

I ought to be ashamed of myself for not writing oftener to you, and have no excuse to offer, except that I am an awfully bad hand at letter writing. I am afraid that I will have very little news to tell you.

I like New Caledonia very much as far as the climate goes, but there is no amusements of any kind. We get up in the morning at five, go to the store at six (having a cup of coffee before going down) & work till a quarter to eleven, when we go home to break-fast, returning to the store between twelve and one & work till six. At seven we have dinner (only two meals a day) and generally go straight to bed, so that you may say, our life here is nothing but eat-ing, drinking, sleeping, & working. Certainly we have a band which plays on Thursday nights and Sunday afternoons. The band is com-posed of convicts, who do nothing else but play, consequently they play splendidly. Howard has got a splendid little house to live in, about the best here. I have only got a dirty little room in an hotel, with not even a chest of drawers to put my things in. We both take our meals at the club, & I must say, they feed us splendidly.

Howard is away in Sydney, but I am expecting him back again by the first steamer, which should be in sometime during the week. I am living in his house whilst he is away, to look after it for him. It is a fearful place for robberies, nearly every night there are some stores and private houses broken into. However we have been won-derfully lucky, as they have never troubled us once. I always am the last to leave the store, & so, see that it is properly fortified, then I have built a house *myself* in the yard, in which, I have at least half a dozen "boys" (as all canaques are called never mind what age they are) to sleep every night. Howard's, house I also look after, well, & I pity any-one that attempts to get in whilst I am staying their. In the yard I have two good watch-dogs loose all night, also two or three boys to sleep outside. In the house I see to everything being "made-fast" myself and have the two little boys (youngsters about ten years of age, Howard has three of them, & no-one else to keep the house in order, & you would be surprised to see how well they do it) each one sleeping across the doors. For myself I have my revolver under my pillow, & I fancy that a thief would receive a warm reception.

Last night, or rather this morning about two oclock, I heard someone trying to open one of the doors. I got up quietly & sneaked along on my hands & knees until I arrived at the opposite door, when through the glass window I saw a head. I took aim at it (for my motto here is - "shoot first, and sing out afterwards") & had my hand on the trigger to shoot, when I noticed that the head was wooley, so I knew that it must be a canaque so I sang out & got for an answer "Its me master." It was one of the little boys, who was trying to open one of the doors, without waking me, but couldn't. Poor little beggar I do not think he quite understood how near he was being shot. He is my favorite boy, not more than ten years old, & has only come from the New Hebrides about a month ago. He is such a pretty little fellow & is just beginning to talk English. I did not sleep a wink afterwards thinking how near I had been to killing the poor little devil. Our cashiers house was broken into last Thursday evening whilst he & his wife were at the band they were not away twenty minutes (between eight & nine oclock) but when they came back the house was turned upside down & everything of value taken, which I am afraid they will never see again. They are sure to give Howard's house a turn, as he has so many valuables. I am only afraid that it will get robbed in the day time, as there are only the two little boys (Howard has the other one in Sydney with him) to look after it. I am not afraid of the night-time whilst I am their.

We have had a most horrible fever here (not dangerous) called "The Dengue," & I fancy nearly everybody has had it. I was one of the first to get it & was bad for more than three weeks. For ten days I eat nothing at all & consequently was too weak to stand, however I was only away from the store for 4 days. Howard, was one of the last to get it, but he was laid up at home for more than a week. We have had no rain for nine months, which made it a great deal worse for the fever. To-day however it is quite cold & raining hard, which should wash away what little there is left of the fever. For the countries sake I hope that it will rain for at least a fortnight.

We spent a miserable Christmas here, being all sick with the "Dengue." Seven of us Englishmen had breakfast together, but it was very dull, for none of us could eat & it was a broiling hot day, after breakfast I went home & lay in a bath all afternoon.

New Years Eve, I and the captain of our schooner went out into the country, & eat our breakfast with a German Family, & spent a pleasant day. You may be sure that I did not forget those at home.

Our schooner is in the "labour trade," that is, she goes down to the islands, gets canaques, they have to come of their own free will (the government have their agent on board to see that everything is done lawfully) & you have to pay their friends for them either in muskets, money, powder &ct. When the ship is full, she returns to Nouméa & their you sell them to whoever likes to buy them for domestiques &ct. Some of them are engaged for 3, 4 & 5 years. The longer they are engaged for, the more money you can get for them. Some of them we got as much as £30/-/- a head for them. The buyer has to give them wages at the rate of, from 9 to 12 francs per month, but does not pay them until their engagement is finished. Everything is done through the Government who see that the canaques are not cheated, at the end of their engagement they have to be returned to their Island.

There is any amount of danger for the ship in going amongst the Islands, as every time a ship comes back we hear of ships being fired at & white men killed by the canaques, & often eaten.

I intended to have gone in our schooner this trip, but it is now the hurricane season, (& people seem to think that we are going to have one this year) so I thought that I would put off my trip, for even if we should be caught in a hurricane & blown ashore, it is poor consolation to be eat, after you have run the risk of swimming ashore &ct. The Frenchmen, here, lost a fine man-of-war about a week ago, she ran on to a reef during the night; luckily there were no lives lost. I do not get on with my French as well as I should, there is too much English spoken here.

Well! I fancy that I have written all I can, & hoping that you are in the best of health & with kind love to all.

Believe me
Ever your loving son,
V. Lee Walker.

I wonder when I shall be able to take a trip home to see you all.

"Willie" is in Australia now, but I am afraid that I will not be able to see him, as Howard will go to Sydney again, when he arrives their & we cannot very well, both leave together. Luck seems to be against me.

Commentary

The "things" that have "changed greatly" are conjugal as well as financial. The woman that Howard brought out to Sydney only the year before has returned, whether before or after they were married is not clear. Does Louie leave simply because Howard's business fails? Why does Lee subsequently "see very little" of Howard?

These letters, of course, are full of silences. Walker's sexuality is one of them; it is an area we would not expect to find any explicit, or even implied, discussion of in letters to his mother. He presents himself as being so isolated that I sometimes wonder if he was celibate. One can only guess why Louie might have thought badly of him or considered him uncouth. Did he make some kind of pass at her that alienates him from Howard as well? Or is Walker only expressing a preoccupation of his own, with his remoteness from decent society? This sense of distance is manifest not only in this awkwardness or rupture, not only in Walker's sense of the improbability of a trip home, but also in his discomfort even in town society in New Caledonia. Noumea, which he appeared previously to enjoy, is now so miserable and beastly that he says the place makes him physically ill. In the letter of July 1884, Walker presents himself as solitary to the point of being silent; by early 1885 this stark isolation is somewhat ameliorated, as he seems to dine with Howard at the club and spend some time visiting with the Irish captain of their labor-trading vessel.

In all of these letters, spanning nearly ten years, there is only a single passage in which Walker expresses any individualized feeling for an islander. He is evidently appalled by how nearly he comes to shooting his houseboy, "a poor little devil," his "favorite boy," "a pretty little fellow." He has shifted a long way since his visit to Fiji, when he remarks on the strangeness of being surrounded by "niggers." I cannot assume that the familiarity that displaced this sense of oddness and distance included sexual relations with either men or women, girls or boys. We do know that many white traders of the period would have entered into such relations, but can only speculate, perhaps pointlessly, about this man's experience. His rough work and heavily tanned skin do not seem quite sufficient to explain his sense that he has become unfit for life "at home."

January 3rd 1886
Nouméa

My dear mother,

I ought to be thoroughly ashamed of myself for not having written to you lately, & there is no excuse for it.

I have just returned from a trading trip to the New Hebrides as super-cargo on board our schooner. Our last super-cargo was killed by the natives & when the schooner returned we could not find a man to fill his place, as it is a rather difficult position to fill. I told Howard that I was sure I could do it better than anyone else, & that I would go for him. He seemed to think that I was not capable, but at the last moment when he could get nobody else to go, he told me to go.

I rather surprised him when I returned two weeks earlier than he thought I could do the trip in. I made a better trip than anyone who had gone down before me.

I can get along with natives better than most people & have no fear of them.

You would hardly know me now, I am more than brown almost black from the sun. Clothes do not trouble one much in the Islands. Pajama trousers & singlet are full dress, always bare-footed, as I am in the water nearly all day jumping from the boat ashore.

In going ashore one has always to be armed to the teeth. I am the only white man that goes ashore from the ship, the others captain and mate (only three white men on board) stay on board to look out for the ship. I always have four boys (all black fellows are called "boys" down here) to pull me ashore, each armed with a rifle & I with a revolver. We back the boat ashore so as to be able to pull away quickly in case of trouble with the natives. I jump ashore & the boat pulls away a short distance the boys all ready with their rifles to cover me. The first thing on landing I am surrounded with from 100 to 300 (according to the place) natives all armed with muskets, rifles, or bows & poisened arrows. They are too frightened of a white man to attack him when they see he is armed, it is only when they see that they can kill you, without any danger to themselves, that they attempt it. I find from experience that the ones that are the worst are those that have been to the white man's country and can speak English, they are the biggest rogues & the ones to be most carefully watched. The one that speaks to you the fairest is the one that will be the first to lift [h]is hand to kill you, or to start the others to do it. I never trust one of them, & always treat them fairly, the consequence is that I can do with natives, more than any one else. A mistake people make is in thinking that they understand the word "gratitude," there is no such word in *their* dictionary, & nobody knows it more than I do, for if any "boy" here gets into trouble I am the first one they come to. The other day one of our "boys" came to me with a fearful wound, he had got it in a fight. I took him to the hospital & got it sewn up for him. A little time afterwards I wanted some night-work done at the store, when he was the only one who refused to come & give a hand.

The life on board these small schooners is not a very happy one bags of rice for a mattress & a blanket, was my bed & after you get "copra" on board it is impossible to sleep below because of the heat & smell, then the hard deck & a blanket consists of my bed, pleasant in bad or rainy weather.

Meals, we have to take as best we can, but always on deck as there is no room down below, & our food as you can imagine is not of the grandest. However in fine weather it is not so very bad, & there is a kind of fascination in the risks you run.

One of our traders had his house burnt down & lost about £150 /-/-'s worth of copra & trade, besides having two shots fired at him, all done by the natives. It happened about four days before I got to his place, since which time he had been sleeping in the bush and living on "yams" &ct. I took him away from the place & fully expected that we would have a fight in leaving, but although there were about 200 of them they were frightened of two white men, & we left without exchanging a shot.

I expected to be in "Nouméa" for Christmas day but when we were quite close we got becalmed & for four days we did not move at all. I was fearfully wild as I wanted to have my Christmas dinner ashore. However, I had bought a pig at my last port of call, in case of accidents, & for fear that we should be at sea for Christmas, so the poor pig had to suffer, & we had fresh meat for dinner, which is a treat for us. I did not forget you at home, & drank all you healthes in a "nobler" of gin, not a very aristocratic drink, but it was all we had on board. New Year's day we had a bachelor's dinner party, & had a pleasant evening of it.

Now I come to think of it, in four more days it will be my birthday, but I cannot for the life of me, think how old I am. It must be somewhere about thirty.

Well! the band has just started to play, so I think that I will go to hear it & try to add a few more lines to this letter another time.
Jan^{ry}.9 2.A.M.
It is too hot to sleep, & as there is a mail leaving at six oclock this morning, I may just as well finish this letter & post it.

I have no more news to add, so with best love to all.

Believe me

Your loving son

V. Lee Walker.

December 25th 1886
At Sea
Off Erromango.

Dear mother

I am thoroughly ashamed of myself for not having written to you for such a long time, but I have been waiting, waiting, waiting to see if the time would not come, when I could write good news, but I am afraid that it will be a long time before I shall be able to do that.

Things have not been going so well with us as they might have done, but I suppose that you will have had all news from Howard so I will only write about myself.

To-day, being Christmas day, of course my thoughts naturally turn to-wards home, and: after lying on my back nearly all morning (too hot to do anything) I thought that I would write a letter home, although I had no good news.

I am at sea, on board a small schooner of 50 tons, on my way to Nouméa, after a voyage round the New Hebrides, to arrange all my affairs, as I have plenty of land and a store their, and I do not know when I may be able to come down here again.

For the last eighteen months I have been living on board this small schooner, all the time in the New Hebrides coming from one Island to the other, selling trade, collecting copra &ct, & when the ship is full taking it to Nouméa & then bringing fresh trade down again. It is a very rough life but I do not dislike it, certainly you have not got much comfort on board, for instance sometimes when short of water we cannot even get a wash for perhaps a week. Dress does not trouble one much, a pair of trousers & singlet, nothing else. My arms, feet, and face, are nearly as dark as a natives, from sunburn. There is a fascination about the live. You never know one minute but you might get knocked on the head by a tomahawk, or shot at with rifle by the natives, as they are all armed. The man whose place I took in the vessel was speared by the natives and killed; I had been with him the trip before. However all the time that I have been in the Islands I have never had any trouble with the natives and have always got on well with them. I am more frightened of fever than of being killed by natives. I suffer a good deal from fever and ague, one time I thought that I was never going to get up again. This trip I have had it bad for a week, but I am nearly well again now. It is strange that I spent last Christmas I spent at sea close to where I am now. We should have been in Nouméa now but got caught in a storm about a week ago & had four of our sails blown away so that we had to put back & anchor, in order to repair sails. We made another start yesterday (rather hard lives, having to go to sea on Christmas eve, but we have to push along as we are behind time). We are now about thirty miles from an island called Erromango, with hardly a breath of wind and a smooth sea. We are just going to have our Christmas breakfast I expect that you would call it dinner, as it is eleven oclock. We have got a grand feed to-day, and all of us have been giving a hand to cook. There are four of us white men on board, Captain, Mate, 1 passenger and myself, 6 natives as crew (they are having a great feast also, to-day) 2 native passengers and a Malabar cook. We have a cold fowl, roast leg of goat and a jam roll. They are calling me on deck to breakfast or Ki-Ki, as it is called here. After Ki-Ki I will continue my letter.

We had just finished our Ki-Ki when there was a cry of shark, two big ones were following the ship, so I got a shark hook and rope, and soon had one of them on deck, he was not a very big one only about 9 or 10 feet long. I put two bullets through his head and cut his tail off, and after all he managed to get over the side of the vessel again. He took charge of the deck whilst we had him on board. One of the boys lost the shark hook overboard, so we could not catch the other one. I afterwards shot a porpoise, so that we have had some sport this afternoon. I am afraid that we are going to have a very long trip to Nouméa, as there is very little wind however I hope to be there before New Years day.

It is now 8.P.M, I suppose about 10.A.M. with you, I wonder what you are all doing, I hope that you all will have a happy Christmas: I wonder *when* I shall spend a Christmas with you again.

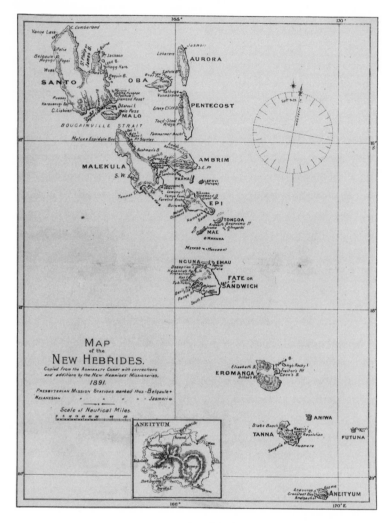

"Map of the New Hebrides, copied from the Admiralty Chart with corrections and additions by the New Hebrides' Missionaries," 1891. National Library of Australia, Canberra.

We could not eat any dinner to-night, as we all got a little fever, but hope to be all well by the time we reach Nouméa. The crew are singing carols for us, whilst I write. They are Maré boys, from the Loyalty Islands. You would be surprised to hear how well they sing. They can all read and write having been taught by an English Missionary, who had spent most of his life on the Island. They can sing better than most white people.

We have got nothing to drink on board but some old tom gin, however I am going to drink all your healths before I turn in. You would be amused if you were to see our cabin. It is about eight feet by six feet, and there are five of us to sleep in it. I can tell you that with the heat of the copra, it is pretty warm. You cannot sleep on deck on account of the fever.

You will wonder that I like this life, but when I get to Nouméa this time I do not know what I shall do, now that Howards business has failed, I am afraid that I will not be able to come down here again.

Howard wants me to go home, but what is the use of my going home, after being down here for so long, I would be fit for nothing at home. Certainly I want to go home to see you all again, but then I would like to pay my own expenses and come back again. Howard says that he is going home as soon as he has settled all his affairs. I am very glad of it, as he has not been well for a long time. I wish that I could see my way to remain down here, but my land will have to remain idle & my store empty until I see if something will turn up.

Howard came down with me last trip, and we managed to get shipwrecked, the ship and cargo was totally lost but luckily no lives. We had to remain on one of the Islands (luckily it was where the troops were stationed, so that we had nothing to fear from the natives) for six or seven days until another vessel took us on to Nouméa.

It is a long time since I commenced this letter, & I have never had time to finish it.

Strange to say I am now again on my way to the New Hebrides, and this time I am going to stop down. I have some stores on board and am going down to finish my store and open it. I shall have plenty of work to do for the first few months and have got four natives with me, to give me a hand.

I will write to you again as soon as I get settled & will tell you how the life suits me. With love to all and trusting that you are all in good health.

Believe me
Ever your loving son
V. Lee Walker

Colonists of diverse kinds and in diverse ways tried to make places of settlement like home, or better than home. Such efforts presupposed the transformation of lands and peoples to bring them into some kind of conformity with European values. But there is a set of risks that corresponds with these potential accomplishments: it may instead be the colonizer who is assimilated to the place, or to indigenous society. And this is what Walker understands to happen to him, not in the sense that he adopts a local lifestyle, but in one respect that is more arresting, given the fetishization of skin pigment in the period: "I am more than brown almost black from the sun"; "My arms, feet, and face, are nearly as dark as a natives." "Going native," now a cliché, was then a specter that was equally present in the fiction dealing with the colonial experience in the Pacific:

> McClure nodded. "Don't go black," he advised.
> I laughed at that, and my laugh was well-informed with conviction. I knew indubitably that no matter how great a hold the islands had on me, never would I forget that I was a white man, a member of the dominant race; never would I drift and slacken and grow slipshod in the things that matter. Yet there are men—one finds them on almost every beach in the wide South Seas—who in other days and other climes have held their heads high with the highest, but who now, because of some queer kink in their mental make-up, or perhaps because of some dimly-remembered transgression of the civilised code, have shed their white men's ways and thus drifted by easy stages into the dingy inertia that places them level with the beasts. They live native fashion; in many cases they have native wives. They are not black men, but neither are they white. They have eaten of the lotos, and in the Lands of Always Afternoon they dream their lives away. (Walsh 1982 [1925]: 88)

The scope for failure envisaged here has intellectual, behavioral, and specifically sexual dimensions. One fact that seems to be crucial has less to do, curiously, with color than with memory and certainty: "going black" may or may not be a potentially visible shift, but is in any case a matter of self-conception, of a man's preserving his sense that he is "a member of the dominant race." Though we might have regarded this racism as being, above all, a tissue of genetic assumptions, it seems rather to have depended on a continuing fashioning of the self. What matters, above all, is attention to the "ways" of white men; and this seems not to be a simple activity of adhering unselfconsciously to propensities within oneself, but an effort of cultivation, requiring a constant struggle to avoid becoming slack or slipshod, a struggle that must correct an internal tendency to "drift" and "forget." Whiteness is not a self-evident natural fact, but a condition that must be defended against enemies within.

What is imagined is a crisis specifically of masculine identity, which can be situated in the imperatives and taboos of colonizing missions. Settler colonialism, in particular, is understood as the penetration of darkness, the transformation of virgin forests into fertile pastures or farms, the fertilization of once sterile or barren lands. The dominant sexual metaphor has been remarked on often enough, and the literalization of the metaphor in the sexual relations that many colonists obviously did have with "native women" served to enact and underline the fundamental inequality of the encounter: black women were accessible to white men, but white women were certainly not available to black men. In one sense, then, the fact that one cross-racial coupling but not the other was possible expressed colonial dominance in its most elementary form; but this demonstration of power also prejudiced the integrity of the white self. Particularly if there was a longer-term re-lationship, the colonizing actor's membership in "decent" white society was inevitably compromised; even if living "native fashion" really meant living in a peculiarly "hybridized" way, specific to a beach community or some other margin between white and indigenous society, the coherence and self-reliance of the colonist as a purely white actor was nevertheless undone. The notion that involvement with local women epitomized degradation and led to tragic conflicts has a long history in the Pacific, and was expressed, for example, not long after Walker's death in many of Louis Becke's stories, in-cluding one entitled *His Native Wife*.

If we take it for granted that racism rested on a genetic construction of identity—the children of white people were white—we would be neglecting a significant dimension of European debate about the nature and causes of physical differences. One of the longest-running arguments in what might broadly be called anthropological thought concerned the extent to which differences in skin color, hair, and other features were permanent and in-nate, or whether they were more properly seen as traits associated with life in particular climates. The environmentalist view, widely expressed in the eighteenth century, took black people to be black because they lived in the tropics; white men there became darker, and their progeny might eventually become as dark as "negroes." Black people in Europe or North America would conversely gradually become lighter. Much of this discussion, especially in its earlier phases, was highly speculative, abstracted from particular evidence concerning either white people in the tropics or black slaves in America, and avoided anomalies such as relatively light-skinned Asians in the tropics; it seems ironic that a well-meaning but empirically flawed argument against the stability of racial differences should find a kind of proof, centuries after it was first enunciated, in the experience of a particular racist settler who declares that he is almost as dark as a native, and so near to being black that his mother would hardly recognize him. His conception of color is evidently similar to that in Walsh's "Romance of New Guinea": one cannot depend on one's whiteness, and though Walsh's character is confident enough that he will retain his, Walker has felt himself slacken.

There is a gap or fissure that seems conspicuous in Walker's identity here; he discovers a kind of value and meaning in particular experiences and conflicts, yet is unable to present this in any positive way. His choice of life figures only negatively, as a lapse or inadequacy that transports him from any better context, that renders him useless in any site of civility. As was noted above, a number of writers, to the contrary, saw the frontier as a site for actions of special value, as a place where a strong and aggressive male pioneer could display himself—usually by doing a good deal of shooting. Walker does not avoid this imagery despite the possibility that it will offend or trouble his mother: he refers quite directly to the risks and the violence and leaves one surprised by how precisely he anticipates his own violent death.

No doubt many colonizing ventures were marked by moments of failure and disappointment. In one district officer's diary from central Fiji, many entries read simply "Still raining. No mail." Missionaries and administrators might lose faith in what they were compelled to impose, or they might realize that "the natives" were adroitly deferring to white dominance in unimportant ways while getting on with their concerns and ancestral religion much as before. Planters and traders might see the value of their petty commodities falling, might despair the corrosion of their bodies by tropical diseases, and might disown their half-caste children. Some of these failures left colonists intact; in other cases, they undid them, leaving them with no more than pieces of experience and value that could not be reconciled.

Bellevue Station
Port Sandwich
Mallicolo
Xmas day 1887,[2]

My Dear Mon,

It is my very painful duty to advise you of the death of Lee.

He left here on the 16th for the Island of Pentecost where I have a large property, after visiting this place, he went up the coast to purchase yams, & landing at Steep Cliff Bay, (or rather he did not land at all) as soon as the boat touched the shore about 100 natives fired on him, he had a couple of shots with his Winchester & was then shot in the arm, & tomahawked at the back of the head, the whole affair did not take two minutes & I think he died without pain. The little vessel could render no assistance as they had only the one boat, but they fired about 100 shots, they were about a mile away. Next day they fell in with a Fiji vessel & went ashore in two boats, the natives had all cleared, but they recovered Lees body, it had not a stitch of clothing on & was simply hacked to pieces, two fingers gone (evidently to get his ring), the body was bought on here & buried in the French Soldier's quarters, all hands turning out. The soldiers went to great trouble over the matter clearing a passage of half a mile through the bush to enable us to have a clear way to the burying ground.

As you may imagine this has been a great shock to me, I have been in bad health for a long time, & it has been a great strain on my weak nerves, & I have been in bed the last two days.

This upsets all my plans, I finished my affairs in New Caledonia, & was only filling in my time until April when I was going home, now Goodness Knows when I will be able to leave here, as I have no white man with me, & have about 40 niggers working on this plantation, & 20 more on another plantation a few miles from here; this place does not suit my health at all.

"Beach at Steep Cliff Bay, Raga, New Hebrides." From an album of photographs by John Beattie, *The Scenery and Peoples of the Islands of the South and Western Pacific* [1906?]. National Library of Australia, Canberra.

I was surprised to see the work Lee had done since I was last here, we have got Coffee, Maize & Tobacco growing, all Kinds of vegetables - over 100 pigs, any amount of Turkeys, Fowl &ct - & it seems very hard that he should be taken away just as he was commencing to make headway.

I am packing up his private effects, & will send them on to you in due course.

Now, my dear Mon, I leave it to you to break the news to our Mother & relations, I do not write to Will as he takes no notice of my letters, & I cannot help saying that if he had acted in anything like a brotherly manner you would have had Lee with you today, it was dead against my advice that Lee ever came to live here, but what was the poor fellow to do, when those who were in a position to help him would not lend a helping hand.

I am sending a report to H.B.M. Consul at Nouméa, & also to the English men of war, but the English will do nothing.

I have got two vessels placed at my disposal one American flag & the other Danish & we intend to go to Pentecost & get our revenge, I have got 20 volunteers here, all white men, splendid shots & accustomed to the Islands, & I expect [an]other 20 from Nouméa & being under foreign flags no-one can interfere with us, & we will make it hot for the natives.

Lee had a crew of 4 niggers, I fancy all were killed but only one body was found, they were all armed, the boat of course was plundered & all arms & trade & a Kenworth about 500frs. The boat which belonged to me & worth 1000frs, was broken up, & burned, so what with the niggers (who belonged to one) &c I make a smart loss - the previous trip Lee made he lost a boat worth 1000 frs.

It is very hard times for one, but I try to keep my pecker up, & must do the best I can until I can get assistance: things have been looking better for me here of late, & I have a good chance of getting a Comp[an]y formed in Melbourne to take over my Estates, I am working with the Missionaries who are now subsidizing a steamer to run between Melbourne & here, & for which I am agent. We have had 20 vessels in here this month, so you will see there is always something doing.

I have about 20 people here to dinner today many being asked long ago by Lee, & who of course did not know of his death, I am afraid it will not be a very merry affair, but I must do my best.

I hope you are all well, & wish you all a happy & prosperous 1888.

Believe me, my Dear Mon,

Your affec. brother

H. Walker

Address letters to Nouméa - my Agent will forward.[3]

Photograph portrait of Louis Becke. Mitchell Library,
State Library of New South Wales, Sydney.

❋ A man's true character is generally revealed by sudden misfortune.[1]

Louis Becke was not a retiring man. He did not allow fate to dictate his fortune, nor an older brother to define his character. Compared to Walker, Becke was a confident man. He did not allow circumstances to overwhelm him, but utilized what he found in the world to his own ends. And yet he was not a successful man. He was more assertive in attempting to fulfill his ambitions, yet his career as a colonist comprised a series of failures and misfortunes and had to be abandoned. Because of his gift for spinning a good yarn, Becke became a more consequential figure than Walker, and yet, even here, his talents did not lead to prosperity. It seems that Becke was not backward in his relations with women either, and yet each of the three relationships we know of seems to have foundered. Becke enjoyed a period of fame, and perhaps many women, but at the end of his life he lived in a hotel room, alone, poor, and alcoholic.

Becke's letters and his later writings are to be understood in the context of the ideas then current. Until recently, studies of the colonization of the Pacific have tended to focus on the ways the colonized were represented by the colonizers: Specifically, to justify the domination and exploitation that occurred with colonization. It was also understood that the racist discourses of the past often rested on the idea of an evolutionary progress through degrees of civilization. There was, however, little recognition of what it meant that the colonizers themselves were imagined as fitting into this racial and cultural hierarchy. It is an interesting point that although the colonizers in general were seen as being at the top of the hierarchy, individual whites were not. Only with the more recent move toward seeing colonial cultures as not "monolithic or omnipotent" has it been realized that the colonizers could fall disgracefully from their position at the top of the hierarchy (Cooper and Stoler 1989: 609).[2] The letters of Becke and Walker demonstrate that colonizers were not always, as they have usually been depicted, astute and successful exploiters of the colonized. Both sets of letters illustrate tellingly what Cooper and Stoler have referred to as the tensions of empire (1989 and see Stoler and Cooper 1997). They give us converse images of failure—

(FOR THE BULLETIN.)

In 188— I was sent by my "owners" to an island in the S.W. Pacific where they had a trading business, the man in charge of which had, it was believed, got into trouble by shooting a native. My instructions were to investigate the rumour, and, if the business was suffering in any way, to take away the trader and put another man in his place. The incident here related is well within the memory of some very worthy men who still dwell under the roofs of thatch in the Western Pacific.

* * *

At the far end, on a native sofa, lay Martin; by his side sat a young native girl fanning him. No one else.

The gaunt black-whiskered trader tried to rise, but with a varied string of oaths lashed together he fell back, waving his hand to me in recognition. The girl was not a native of the island—I could see that at a glance. She was as handsome as a picture, and, after giving us a dignified greeting, in the Yap (Caroline Islands) dialect, she resumed her fanning and smoking her cigarette.

"Martin," I said, "shake yourself together. What is the matter? Are you sick, or is it only the usual drunk?"

"Both," came in tones that sounded as if his inside were lined with cotton wool; "got a knife in my ribs six months back; never got well; and I've been drinking all the time"—and then, with a silly smile of childish vanity, "all over her. She's my new girl, wot d'ye think of her. Ain't she a star?"

All this time Chaplin stood back until I called him up and said to the trader, "Our new captain, Martin?"

"By God," said the trader, slowly, "if he ain't the image of that —— nigger-catching skipper that was here from Honolulu four year ago."

"That's me!" said Chaplin, coolly puffing away at his cigar, and taking a seat near the sofa with one swift glance of admiration at the face of the girl.

* * *

got to give up this girl or get away from the island. Now, I don't want to make any man feel mean, but she don't particularly care about you, and——"

The graceful creature nodded her approval of Chaplin's remarks, and Martin glared at her. Then he took a drink of gin and meditated. Two minutes passed. Then Martin turned.

"How much?" he said.

"Fifty pounds, sonny. Two hundred and fifty dollars."

"Easy to see you've been in the business," mumbled Martin; "why, her mother's worth that. 'Tain't no deal."

"Well, then, how much *do* you want?"

"A hundred."

"Haven't got it on board, sonny. Take eighty sovereigns and the rest in trade or liquor?"

"It's a deal," said Martin; "are you game to part ten sovereigns for the girl's mother, and I'll get her back from the natives?"

"No," said Chaplin, rising; "the girl's enough for me."

She had risen and was looking at Martin with a pallid face and set teeth, and then without a word of farewell on either side she picked up a Panama hat and, fan in hand, walked down to the boat and got in, waiting for Chaplin.

* * *

in double-quick time the whaleboat was lowered and search was made. In half-an-hour Chaplin returned, and gaining the deck said, in his usual cool way, to the mate: "Hoist in the boat and fill away again as quick as possible." Then he went below.

A few minutes afterwards he was at his accustomed amusement, making tortoise-shell ornaments with a fret-saw.

"A sad end to the poor girl's life," I said.

"Yes," said the methodical ex-Honolulu blackbirder, "and a sad end to my lovely five hundred dollars."

LOUIS BECKE.

Extract from "A Dead Loss," Louis Becke, *Bulletin*, 15 December 1894,
p. 19. National Library of Australia, Canberra.

of the inability of some colonizers to shape the world according to their own aspirations.

Like Walker's, Becke's letters from the colonial periphery of the Pacific in the 1880s were addressed to his mother, telling her of his life as a trader. Although he was a bad colonist, Becke at least escaped with his life, and his experiences were to be of profit to him as the basis for his Pacific tales. Despite his widespread popularity at the turn of the century, however, Becke is now an almost forgotten literary figure. All the same, his many books and writings constitute a substantial record of the kinds of thought and the practices that occurred during the nineteenth-century colonization of the Pacific.

Considerably more is known about Becke than about Walker, who can be known only from the fragments that can be excavated from his letters. Nevertheless, Becke is something of a puzzle, for in attempting to come to grips with his character one constantly finds that the images he projects of himself are fraught with contradiction. Thus, despite the availability of far more source material, the portrait we can construct seems to be inconsistent. We will argue that there is a reason for this inconsistency: Becke is seeking to construct himself according to the current ideals of masculinity as they were played out in the context of colonialism.

Born George Lewis Becke at Port Macquarie in New South Wales on June 18, 1855, the son of a clerk of petty sessions, Becke preferred to be known by the name of Louis.[3] Like many boys of that era he had probably heard and been enthralled by tales of adventure on the high seas, and he was reputed to have desired as a boy to become a pirate. It is an ironic coincidence that Becke was later to be charged with piracy (although the charges were dismissed as unfounded).

Becke's long association with the Pacific began before his seventeenth birthday when, in March 1872, he expressed his yearning for adventure by stowing away on a ship bound for Samoa. There he disembarked and found work in a store. For the next twenty years, interspersed with some time in Australia, Becke worked in the Pacific as a supercargo, trader, and labor recruiter.[4] He worked as supercargo on the *Leonora* for Captain "Bully" Hayes, who was notorious throughout the Pacific as a pirate, con man, and thief, an almost legendary status that was to be greatly enhanced by Becke's writings. In 1874 the vessel traded in the northwest and central Pacific until March that year, when it was wrecked at Kusaie. The crew was stranded for six and a half months before being rescued. Becke spent much of this time in a Kusaiean village well away from Hayes—according to Becke, because of the way Hayes and some of his companions were treating the local inhabitants. When a British warship arrived, Hayes escaped but Becke was charged with piracy and taken to Australia because of the questionable way Hayes had obtained the *Leonora*.[5] Becke spent a considerable part of the next few years in Australia, although exactly how much is unclear. He continued to pursue adventure, participating in the Palmer River gold rush and working on a station in Queensland and as a clerk in Townsville.

In early 1880 Becke returned to the islands, remaining at least until late 1882, the period documented in the letters reproduced here. During this time he worked, as an independent trader and for three different firms, in the Gilbert and Ellice Islands, New Britain, and the Marshall Islands. This was a period of considerable change and great adventure, which will be explored more fully in the commentary that accompanies the letters. It seems probable that Becke remained in the Marshall Islands from the time of the last letter, sent from there in November 1882, until he returned to Australia probably in 1886, when he was married. Both he and his wife, Mary Elizabeth Maunsell, visited the islands, but she became ill and they returned to Australia, with Becke returning alone to the islands intermittently.

Becke finally left the islands permanently to live in Sydney in 1892. Popular knowledge has it that in Sydney he was introduced to J. F. Archibald, the founder and editor of the *Bulletin*, by Ernest Favenc, another author and friend, and thus began his literary career. He had, though, been working as a journalist for a year prior to this event. It is said that after hearing some of Becke's stories, Archibald urged that he write them down. His first short story, "Bully Hayes: The Pirate of the Pacific," appeared in the *Bulletin* in 1893, and his first collection, *By Reef and Palm,* was published in 1894, to be reprinted three times in that year. It was his long association with the Pacific that gave Becke the wealth of experience and adventure that forms the backbone of his tales, giving them a vivid and realistic complexion. Over the next two decades he was to write thirty-four books (including six novels in collaboration with Walter Jeffery, the editor of *Town and Country Journal*). His titles included *Bully Hayes: Buccaneer, The Ebbing of the Tide, Under Tropic Skies, Ridan the Devil and Other Stories, The Adventures of Louis Blake,* and *His Native Wife.* In 1896, Becke left for Europe, where he lived mainly in England, also spending some time in Ireland and France. In 1909 he returned to Australia, where he died in 1913. Besides his fiction, he produced numerous articles and journalistic pieces for magazines and newspapers and had a regular column, "London Notes," in the *Sydney Evening News,* where he reported items of interest and trivia concerning various celebrities and authors.

Letters from the Colonial Periphery

The ten letters reproduced here were written by Becke from the Equatorial Pacific, the region that today is referred to as Micronesia. Most of them were written while he was a trader in the Ellice Islands (now called Tuvalu) or in transit to other islands of Micronesia, such as the Gilbert Islands or Kingsmill Group (now called Kirabati) and the Marshall Islands. Encompassing the period from April 11, 1880 to November 1, 1882, they are a scattered collection with obvious interruptions in continuity. Although he mentions the terrible time he had in New Britain in one letter, no letters from there have survived. Like the letters of Walker, they are not rich texts of great value to the more conventional historian. Rather, they are a small collection of incomplete writings, concerned with practicalities such as the comings and goings of shipping and the best way to maintain communication. Scant in detail, they are fragmentary and disorderly, giving only brief glimpses and rare snatches into the life of the trader. Letters such as these, however, open up another dimension in our understanding of the history of colonialism in the Pacific. Their fragmentation and partial nature can be read as revealing the fragmentary and partial nature of colonization and of the colonists themselves. Becke's letters, like Walker's, capture the ups and downs of the trader's life, the gains and losses. In addition, with the help of the hindsight provided by his later writings, it is possible to discern in Becke's letters an effort to construct himself in a mold that conforms to the ideals of the times.

Far from fulfilling the initial optimism of the first letter, where Becke predicts that he will make money, the letters catalogue a never-ending series of disasters. The disasters Becke confronts, such as a hurricane and a shipwreck, can be seen, in a wider sense, as metaphors for the failure Becke was to become as a trader. Far from constructing what Shapiro (1988: 58) has termed an explicit personal success narrative of the trader profiting on the colonial frontier, Becke's letters constitute what could be described as an explicit personal failure narrative. His letters catalogue not his successes but his financial ruin, his life in the Pacific as a bad colonist.

If we get a picture of colonialism as not particularly successful, we also get a picture that is complex, wrought by many competing forces. For example, the interests and agendas of the traders and the government agents who oversee the activities of their nationals in the Pacific do not always coincide. As an Australian in the Pacific, Becke is subject to British laws, laws that he decries as overly restrictive. Far from being unencumbered by regulation, trade here is constrained and impeded. In one letter, Becke speaks nostalgically of the past before British regulation and wishes he were an American, exempt from it. The intrusion of imperial control is not uniform; it is not successfully applied by the colonizers, but is lax and piecemeal. As a result, Becke and his colleagues had everything stolen from them by islanders whom he was later to characterize as "intractable." However, it is the Royal Navy, which Becke disparages as part of the control system, that intervenes to punish the islanders responsible (see below). This contradiction shows that Becke is articulating different perspectives according to the varying circumstances in which he writes. Similarly, Becke's disparagement of some traders but not others shows the extent to which the traders themselves can be seen not as a homogeneous bloc, but as separated by competing aims. It becomes more apparent in Becke's Pacific tales that these divisions are often linked to questions of class.

Despite their differences, there are some striking similarities between the letters of Becke and those of Walker. As we have argued of Walker, Becke's letters are characterized by a notable absence of description of the environment in which he is located, descriptions that would make the unfamiliar more accessible to the reader. Like Walker, Becke avoids evoking a landscape of aesthetic affect, preferring to recount some of the unusual incidents of his daily life. This is surprising in Becke, particularly as his later writings contain many romantic renderings of the Pacific landscape (a landscape often spoiled by the intrusion of unsavory colonists). Mostly, the concerns and events he recounts center on Becke himself and point to the ways in which he authors himself through these texts. Further, apart from his account of navigation by fire, there is little ethnographic reportage. The islands are presented as a rather incomprehensible place and the islanders as rather incomprehensible beings, a cultural and ethnographic void, with few gestures toward understanding the other.[6] In sum, not only do Becke's letters reveal some of the wider tensions within the colonizing cultures in the Pacific, the tensions of empire, they also reveal the process by which colonizers such as Becke seek to fashion themselves as a particular kind of colonist and man.

Through their descriptions of historical events, empiricist historians seek to portray the objective reality of events in the narrative texts they weave. In seeking to describe the "way it really was," they mostly eschew "fictional" texts. Biographers of Becke have often remarked on the disparity between the accounts of his life he offers for literary consumption through his narrative tales and what really happened. Disparities have even been noted in his accounts of his life in supposedly nonfictional texts. As a number of commentators have noted, the biographical introduction to his first collection of short stories, *By Reef and Palm,* written by Lord Pembroke and based on notes supplied by Becke, is full of "factual" errors. Others, however, have taken the inverse position. Maude, for example, has remarked that many of Becke's so-called fictions are based on real events: "The division made between fiction and non-fiction writing is, however, rather artificial and disguises the fact that Becke based much, probably most, of his so-called fiction on the stories of actual events which he heard recounted by the traders and natives with whom he mixed, supplemented by library research" (1967: 226). It would be a great shame to dismiss Becke's "fiction" as of limited use because the factual details are often erroneous. Equally, it would be a great shame to accept his letters unproblematically as "nonfiction," given that many of them feature gaps and silences and are constructed so as to represent a particular image of himself to his mother. Although such gaps and silences, disparities and disjunctures may lead the empiricist historian to despair, they can be exceedingly illuminating. Rather than a homogeneous truth, the disjunctures, ruptures, gaps, and silences reveal the complexities and tensions of empire, as well as the ways men, such as Becke, seek to represent themselves in a particular way, which changes over time. This is not to suggest that there are "no facts," but that facts alone cannot portray the complexities of human interactions, and so slide over the realities.

Like Maude, we do not wish to take up the distinction between "nonfiction" or "truth" and "fiction," but rather to suggest that the terrain of writing in the form of letters, like that of short stories, is refracted through the prism of the imagination. In other words, both "fiction" and "nonfiction" are born through imaginings. So, we prefer to take Becke's letters and his later writings as one body of work. If we see both the writing of "nonfiction," such as letters, and the writing of "fictional" short stories or novellas as processes of writing or refashioning the self and the world, then it is possible to gain a greater understanding of the author's way of being in the world, and also greater appreciation of the complexity of colonialism and its contradictions.

This is a world that changes in complex and disjunctive ways. Thus, though there are many differences between his letters and his later writings, there are also similarities. In terms of differences, the letters and his fiction were written during different phases of imperialism. Although written during a period of increased imperial rivalry just prior to the scramble for Africa, the letters were written before official colonial annexation took place in the Pacific. His stories were written later, at a time of interventionary imperialism, a period of intense imperial rivalry that preceded and followed the annexation and imposition of colonial regimes across Africa and the Pacific.[7] Despite these differences of era, there are thematic continuities. Here we have in mind the image of whites "going native" that occurs in both the letters and his Pacific tales (muted in the earlier and more obvious in the later writings).

In both his letters and his Pacific tales, Becke fashions a particular self through the process of writing: a plucky hero struggling against the environment and peoples of the Pacific. He writes himself as the resolute colonist who withstands the temptations to fall while in this foreign environment, unlike so many of those who figure in his writings. It is of interest that Becke's letters lack the alarmist nature of much writing representing the colonial periphery. Unlike his later tales, which are filled with acts of savagery, his letters are constrained, tending to downplay the disasters he confronts. This was no doubt due to his wish not to alarm his mother, particularly because letters either took a long time to reach Australia or went astray. However, by downplaying the enormity of what happens to him, Becke is also presenting an image of himself as a man of fortitude who is ready to face and overcome all the difficulties he confronts. With true pluck he grits his teeth and gets on with life. The disasters he confronts are not for him insurmountable problems that would cause a lesser man to give up in despair, but constitute the challenges of life that test him. A similar kind of self-fashioning is at work in Becke's failure to mention that he married a local woman while on the island of Nukufetau. Through such a silence, Becke writes himself as unlike the typical traders who "go native," crossing the racial and cultural divide by marrying locals, adopting local dress, or behaving as the locals do. Thus, if Walker writes of himself as "going native," then Becke writes of himself as the opposite, as a person who is above this.

If we see letter writing as a process of writing the self, there is some similarity between the processes of letter writing and autobiography.[8] As literary artifacts, both seek to inscribe a particular image of the self. Both processes can be regarded as what Foucault calls techniques of the self, the means by which the self fashions the self for an audience. Thus we do not take the view that the "true self" is disclosed in private communications but is hidden in public. The public and the private self are often different, but this means that the self is not unitary, not that one is real and the other not. On the contrary, private letters, like autobiography, are a part of the process of writing the self, of constructing the self through the word. Letters may not convey the more refined and polished forms of narrative, displaying the coherence and closure of autobiography, but in that lack of closure they can give a more penetrating view of the production of self. We take the view that the self Becke presents to his mother is not a pretense, but is an effort to make himself in that mold.

As we have suggested, the content of Becke's letters to his mother is circumscribed, and what is left unsaid is as revealing as what is said. In much the same way as Shapiro (1988) has suggested for the autobiographical writings of Benjamin Franklin, Becke casts himself as the model most appropriate to the context. The task for Becke, in the words of Shapiro, "became more than simply exemplifying the ideal character; it extended as well to valorising the context within which such a character ought to function" (57). Just as Franklin in his autobiography constructs himself as an advertisement for America, Becke constructs himself as an advertisement for colonialism. Becke values both the context, that is colonialism, in which the ideal character ought to function and the sort of character the ideal colonist ought to embody.

As others have shown, the discourse of character was a pervasive component of imperial and colonial discourse, especially in the nineteenth century. Some, such as Richards (1989), even suggest that it was vital to the British Empire (see also Chakrabarty 1994 and Field 1982). "Good conduct and sound character were more than just desirable," he writes, "[t]hey were essential. They were the justification of the British Empire" (76). An individual with character was thought to possess certain highly valued moral and personal qualities, which were an essential justification for imperialism. The notion of character not only encompasses moral consistency but such things as consistency of action, "self-restraint, perseverance, strenuous effort, [and] courage in the face of adversity" (Collini 1985: 36). Implicit in Becke's letters, the discourse of character is a dominant theme in his Pacific tales. For Becke, to lack character or to have a bad character signals a propensity to degeneracy. The discourse of character that Becke enunciates speaks clearly of the need to maintain racial boundaries. It also shows how in the colonial context the concept of race is saturated with discourses of class.

Becke's encounter with another trader, George Winchcombe, is illuminating in this regard, showing how the trading community was fractured by divisions based in part on class. As we deal more substantially with their encounter and their representations of each other in the commentary on the letters, here we will merely raise some points relevant to our overall argument. In one of his letters Becke says that people like Winchcombe are "no better than the natives." Years later, Becke featured Winchcombe as a character in one of his stories, "Tarria, the Swimmer." Winchcombly, as he is named, is a degenerate white who is so dirty and unkempt that Becke's alter ego, another trader, questions whether he is indeed white. Eventually the treacherous and degenerate Winchcombly is killed off by Becke's alter ego. Winchcombe also gives an account of his meeting with Becke in his diary, this time on the island of Nukufetau and, in much the same way as Becke, he constructs Becke as a dissolute and somewhat unscrupulous character, very different from the picture Becke presents of himself.

Which of their respective accounts is the more "truthful" or embodies the "truth" is not really relevant to the issues we are concerned with here. Rather, we see the disparities and contradictions as pointing to the process of authoring, of writing the self in a particular way. As Becke acknowledges when he argues in a letter that on the whole the trader of today is better than in previous times, the common image of white settlement and trade in the Pacific was one of violence and white degeneracy. Prior to Becke's and Winchcombe's residence, there had been a long history of whites living in

"Began to roll up his sleeves . . . ," illustration by Norman Lindsay, from Louis Becke, *Bully Hayes: Buccaneer and Other Stories*, Sydney: New South Wales Bookstall Co., 1923, p. 101.

the Pacific—escaped convicts, castaways, beachcombers, and traders, who often adopted local dress, had their bodies tattooed, and married local women. Men such as this were thought to have "gone native," to have degenerated to a state of "savagery" like the islanders. There was a prevailing image of the Pacific as a place where whites were scarcely capable of living without losing their cultural and racial identity. It is not surprising that both Becke and Winchcombe should try to distance themselves from that image and from the types of whites who had lived in the Pacific previously. Becke authors himself as one who maintains his racial and cultural integrity, as different from those earlier whites who went "native," of whom he sees Winchcombe to be a latter-day example. But if Becke constructs Winchcombe as one of those vestigial characters from a bygone era, Winchcombe does the same to Becke.

The image of Becke as the morally upright colonist and Winchcombe as the unkempt and degenerate trader is shown in the Norman Lindsay illustration in the 1923 edition of *Bully Hayes: Buccaneer,* which contains the story "Tarria, the Swimmer." Although the face of Becke's alter ego, the trader Watson, is shaded and cannot be said to bear a likeness to Becke, and was created in a later period, it conveys an image of the type of colonist Becke had wanted to present. It shows Watson immaculately dressed in a white (pajama) suit, complete with tie and shoes and, as the archetype of the upright colonist, wearing a white pith helmet. Winchcombly presents the opposite picture. He wears neither shoes nor tie, and his clothes are untidy and worn. Whereas he is presented rolling up his shirt sleeves preparing to fight his adversary, Becke's alter ego, in contrast, stands with his hands on his hips, in a pose clearly illustrating his reserve and coolheadedness in the heat of the situation.

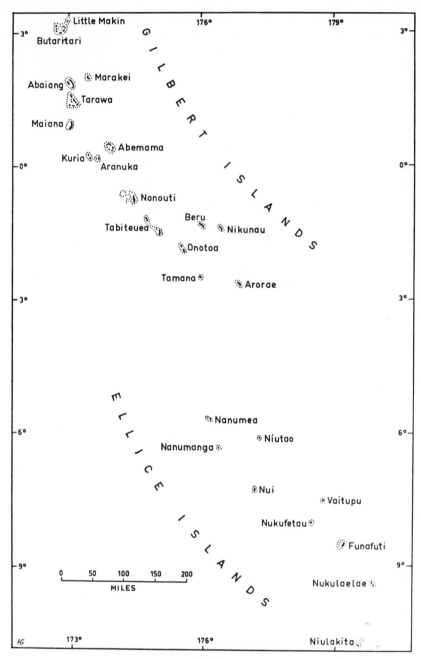

"The Gilbert and Ellice Islands," from Deryck Scarr, *Fragments of Empire*,
Australian National University Press, Canberra, 1967.

Schooner "The Venus"
off the island of
Nanumaga [Nanumanga]
Ellice Group
South Pacific Ocean
April 11th. 1880

My dear Mama

Just a few lines to tell you that I am going to remain on the above island for 18 months and am busy landing my goods. it is called Hudson's island or Nanomaga [Nanumanga] and is a small island with about 200 people on it - and no white men - there is a Samoan teacher here and he and his wife Elina are old friends of mine and I will live with them until my house is built. The king and chiefs have made a law that only one white man is to live on the island and that has decided me to remain as I think I will do very well here - the people are very friendly and I hope in 6 months more to be able to speak their language well - the island is only 3 miles long and is an atoll or a lagoon island - no anchorage - vessels must lie off and on - "The Venus" is coming back for my copra in about 4 months and then she goes to Sydney. I have about three thousand dollars $3000 of trade and I am busy getting it on shore. it is now Sunday and the "Venus" leaves on Tuesday - we cannot land anything to day being Sunday as the natives are great missionaries in their way. When you write to me send to care of Capt Hamilton and write below "Nanumaga" Ellice Group. The chief officer of the Venus Mr Senior is a particular chum of mine and I give him this letter to give to any ship he may meet in the Kingsmill Group.

The native teacher and his wife are such nice people and I am sure I will be very comfortable and make some money.

I will not fail to write and tell you how I get on by every opportu-

Nanumaga. Ellice Group. S. Pacific
February 21.1881.

My dear Mama. I have had a rough time of it since last writing _on the 2d of this month my station was destroyed by a hurricane. For some two or three days previous to this we knew that something strange was to happen, many strange sea-birds unknown to the natives came flying from the westward and with strange cries settled on the beach and on the cocoanut trees, for nearly two months past it had been blowing heavily from the westward, but on the 1st the wind fell and the sea made a curious noise like the bellowing of some beast. Next day it commenced to blow and and my anxiety was great lest the house would give way, but although it withstood the force of the wind it succumbed to a new and unexpected danger. At three o'clock in the morning it then being pitch dark and raining and blowing furiously, and dead low water I was sitting in one of my servants houses with three natives of Dr Bayster's island and some of my workpeople watching my dwelling house was was in danger from two tall cocoa nut trees which every moment threatened to fall and crush in the roof. It was now blowing furiously the air filled with salt spray and as I expected a change at turn of tide. I sent a little girl to crawl along on the sand to the beach and see if the tide was coming in _ in a few minutes she came flying back saying. The sea has gone away, there is nothing but tarevereve (great empty space). Anticipat_ ing something curious we ran into the big house and the next minutes with a strange roaring sound the sea rose up like a wall and dashed over the reef in one mighty wave and swept up into

nity. I must now close up and with love to all at home I am dearest Mother

Your affectionate Son
Louis G. Becke

Commentary

By the time this letter was written the twenty-five-year-old Becke was an old hand, having lived in the Pacific since 1872. His experience of living for six

the village, sweeping away fifteen houses like chaff - the next wave
dashed into my front room and filled it with coral rocks and sand
How glad I am to say that by working like demons we saved all the
trade, or at all events almost everything of value, by the time I had
got everything carried into the rear of the village and out of danger
the wind was at its height and the sound it made was like
the droning of countless flocks of bees, and sea after sea rolled up
into the village, in a few minutes my house, trade house, copra
houses, fowl houses pig houses etc were things that had been, and
were piled up without much regard to regularity in a heap, together
with sundry drowned pigs and other live stock, the next wave they
went went away to sea together with a few native houses. I lost
some copra but saved 7000 lbs and also saved my canoe which is a
valuable one, so altogether I won't grumble, as I might have lost all.
I have written to De W. to tell him of this. I estimate general loss at
$250:00 or $300:00. The natives say it is 35 years since such a storm
as this visited the island. It is now the 21st and you will perhaps be
surprised to know that I am back again in the old position with
new house, copra houses, cook houses, and man servants and maid
servants and all things that are his. Some hundreds of thousands
of young coconuts have been destroyed and I am anxiously awaiting
the arrival of one of our vessels, to consult as to what is to be done.
My vessel is now some five months overdue. I will now say good bye
and with love to all I am dear mama. Your affectionate son, Louis.

Letter by Louis Becke, Nanumaga, Ellice Group, South Pacific, February 21, 1881, two pages. Mitchell Library, State Library of New South Wales, Sydney.

and a half months among the local people on Kusaie in 1874 would have given him a good understanding of life on a small island and how to establish rapport with the local inhabitants—useful experience for settling into the lifestyle of a lone trader on a remote island.

Mainly because the local leaders have restricted the white population to one trader, the tone of this first letter is cheerful and optimistic. Without rivals, he predicts that he "will do very well here," a point that he reiterates toward the end of the letter when he says he will make some money. Like other traders in this region, Becke will be trading much of the $3,000 of goods for locally produced sun-dried copra. Perhaps not wanting to alarm his mother, he does not mention what goods he is trading, probably including guns, ammunition, tobacco, cloth, and possibly liquor, although his employer did not want his employees to trade in this last item (see below). Becke is working for the Liverpool merchant and shipping firm of J. S. De Wolf and Company, one of the many smaller trading firms that had short-lived operations in the Pacific. Attracted by ever-increasing world copra prices, the firm sent *The Venus,* a 191-ton three-masted schooner, to Samoa in 1878, unfortunately for them at a time when the competition was at its fiercest level (Munro 1980: 23–24).[1] Using Apia in Samoa as a base, De Wolf and Company traded beyond there to places such as the Tuamotus, Tonga, the Caroline Islands, and the Gilbert and Ellice Islands, where Becke became its resident trader.

Apart from his enthusiasm about the possibility of making some money, the overall tone of this letter is bland, and it appears to have been written in a hurry. As is the case with many of his letters, it details the comings and goings of shipping and the means by which practical communication with his mother is to be facilitated. This is the letter of a dutiful son, concerned to keep his mother informed and reassured as to his welfare. He tells her twice, for example, that he has good friends on the island, an educated man and his wife, "such nice people," who will make him "comfortable." This is no travel narrative—we get no sense of where he has come from or how he came to be there, and we do not learn of any adventures or interesting people he has met on the way; there are no evocative descriptions of the landscape in which he finds himself or of the local people he is to live with. In his rather uninspired description of the place that is to be his home, Becke does not evoke the South Sea island paradise that has captured the Western imagination. As with Walker's first letter, there is no sense of an aesthetic possessiveness that might accompany his economic exploitation of the island, although Becke's later writings are replete with romantic descriptions of the landscape. In "Ema, the Half-Blood," although he characterizes the Gilbert and Ellice Islands as "the most uninviting and monotonous in appearance" of all "the thousands of islands that stud the bosom of the North Pacific," he also offers a description that is far more striking than that in his first letter. He writes:

> The long, endless lines of palms, stretching from one end of an island to the other, present no change or variation in their appearance till, as

is often the case, the narrow belt of land on which they so luxuriously thrive becomes, perhaps, but fifty yards in width, and the thick matted undergrowth of creepers that prevail in the wider parts of the island gives place to a barren expanse of wind-swept sand, which yet, however, supports some scattered thousand-rooted palms against the sweeping gusts from the westward in the rainy season, and the steady strain of the south-east trades for the rest of the year.

In such spots as these, where the wild surf on the windward side of the island sometimes leaps over the short, black reef, shelving out abruptly from the shore, and sweeps through the scanty groves of palm and pandanus trees, and, in a frothy, roaring flood, pours across the narrow landbelt into the smooth waters of the lagoon, a permanent channel is made, dry at low water, but running with a swift current when the tide is at flood. (1897b: 9–10)

Nanumaga (Hudson's Island)
Ellice Group 8 July 1880

My dear Mama

About ten days ago Willie Williams came here in his vessell a native schooner the "Vaituputemle" he told me that he was in Samoa two months ago and saw Mr De Wolf there and that Captain Hamilton had a lot of letters for me but although Williams offered to take them Capt Hamilton did not give them to him as he had not yet heard from me and did not know whether I was in the Ellice or Kingsmill or Marshall Groups, neither of course did De Wolf as he left "the Venus" at Funajuti [Funafuti] - so my letters are still in Samoa, of course I am sure there is one from you amongst them; however I expect to get them when the "John Williams" comes here in October, that is if I am still here; for in consequence of events that have happened I am thinking of leaving and going away farther to the northward.

I have had a serious dispute with the natives or rather with a chief here and his people and I have closed my trade house and do not now buy any copra and unless they pay me ten thousand cocoa-nuts I will leave the island with my trade as to remain would be a great loss to De Wolf and Sons.

I have built a very large house and outhouses and am or [?] was quite settled down till this affair happened - most fortunately I kept calm although a few more words would have brought on a terrible mess - and I don't want to be taken to Fiji in a man-o-war to make the acquaintance of the estimable Chief Justice Corrie, the High Commissioner for Polynesia, for in all disputes now with natives especially if there is any blood-shed an *Englishman* is run up with a rope with little compunction - a man in the South Seas now might as well be a Chinaman as an Englishman for all the protection he will receive - the first chance I get I will naturalise myself as a citizen of the United States.

Almost all the people on this island like me and are well deposed and friendly to me but I want to go further to the northward where the people are free from that curse of the islands the missionary element, the missionaries have only been here about five years and they have as usual succeeded in rendering the natives less ferocious but ten thousand times more cunning, lying, avaricious and hypocritical than they were in their natural state, and in which the Almighty intended them to remain else he would not permit them to undergo such a change for the worse. Since "the Venus" left me no other vessels have been here except the "Vaitupulemele" - times are very much changed in the islands now no whaleships now cruise in this group. If I can get De W's approval I will try get up to Strongs Island [Kosrae] or else in the Caroline or Marshall Groups. I am living pretty lonely at present as I have dismissed all my workpeople and servants and have kept only a little native girl Pautoe who keeps house for me and cooks for me native fashion and whom I have adopted there is of course a great row going on every day meetings etc and on an average I receive two deputations every day imploring me to remain and not to close my trade house but they might as well cry to a stone. I rise every day at 4. am. and bathe and then Pautoe gets my breakfast generally flying fish or lobsters and fills my pipe (I smoke a pipe now) and cleans the house while I smoke and instruct her on how to use a broom and wash plates etc without breaking more than two at one wash-up, about 10 oclock some 20 or 30 native girls come and sit on the veranda in the shade and plait straw or sinnet and try and wheedle a cigarette out of the white man and as they consider it a great privilege to come and talk to the white man I make them pay for it by bringing me fish, puraka and young cocoanuts to drink. I think I drink about 30 cocoanuts every day - every evening the missionary and his wife Eline send me ten cocoanuts and something for tea and I return the compliment by either a little beef or biscuit or whatever I may have ready at the time. About a month ago I and Felipe a native of Nukufetau (De Peyster Island) built a house on the windward side of the island and lived there with his family in all 8 of us but since this quarrel I have come back to my big house in the village.

Yesterday (Saturday) was a very heavy day to me - there was great meeting of the people and I went to demand my fine - not being well enough acquainted with the language to make my speech I had to do so in Samoan and a Samoan present translated for me - my opponent said little except that he was guilty but could not pay the fine as the people were now paying off a fine of Willie Williams of $500. one hundred and ten thousand cocoanuts; which they are now paying to me as Willie William's deputy as he is to give me 5% on all they pay. So far they have paid on William's a/c 6094 lbs copra about $100. If I was an American or a German I could make the natives pay me about $2500 in copra but as I am an Englishman I can not. I don't expect "the Venus" here now, she must have gone away up into the Carolines or else back to Samoa or is lost, in the latter case you will not receive the letters I gave to young Senior my chum the mate Williams told me that De Wolf was waiting in Samoa for one of his vessells a schooner "the "Redcoat" coming from England with a general cargo - she will I dare say come here to me and then go up to the Line Islands. The weather has been lovely here for some 8 or ten days and next week the missionary and I are going in a canoe to Nanomea to see if we can learn anything of "The Venus" it is distant about 50 miles and of course out of sight as all these Ellice islands are mere sand banks - when a canoe leaves here it starts on a dark night at Sundown - a huge fire is made on the beach and the glare of it is seen in Nanomea, by which the people there know a canoe is coming - and they at once make an answering fire to guide the canoe to them in fair weather it usually takes a canoe ten hours to cross but if the current is strong some days. I would have gone alone long ago but I have no compass. I will leave my house in charge of Pautoe my little girl and expect to be back in 4 days. I have nice little cat given me by the Carpenter of the "Venus" and she is a famous rat-catcher - the natives call her "*the pig with toenails that can climb trees*" and she is much admired and caressed by the native children, her name is "Dodger"

[unsigned]

Commentary

Written some three months after the first in the collection, this letter shows that Becke's original optimism has soured and captures the ups and downs of his relationship with the Nanumangans. Written both during the dispute and after it was resolved, it provides a good illustration of the tenuous nature of trading on the colonial periphery. From his optimistic predictions of staying for eighteen months and prospering, after three months he has dismissed all of his workpeople and servants, is "living pretty lonely," and is contemplating moving elsewhere. The exact nature of the dispute with the island chief is not clear, but it is clear that it is serious enough to cause him, a man who values levelheadedness and self-control, to threaten to leave. The silences in Becke's report suggest that he seeks to author himself as the injured party. This tends to be confirmed when Becke's "opponent" admits he is guilty.

Although violence was avoided because Becke maintained his calm, he makes it clear that he would not have been so restrained if the British government had not been policing the actions of its citizens in the Pacific. If he were not an Englishman, he hints, he would perhaps have had recourse to bloodshed. Unlike many of the Pacific tales in which, through the voice of the narrator, Becke constructs himself as a colonist with character unwilling to use violence to further his interests, this letter speaks of just such a readiness, constrained only by fear of British juridical intervention. For Becke it is obvious that the law should be protecting the commercial interests of the British trader, not defending the interests of the Pacific islanders. This letter conveys a nostalgia for a past when trade in the Pacific was unfettered by regulation.

Becke overestimates the ability of the British government to police citizens such as he. The high commissioner's effective jurisdiction in the waters of the Gilbert and Ellice Islands, as for the Western Pacific more generally, was greatly understaffed and underresourced. This alone severely limited the high commissioner's ability to police British subjects, but there were also considerable legal difficulties in administering laws applicable to subjects outside of British dominions.[2] The prosecutions enacted by the High Commission in the early 1880s, in the main, appeared to be the result of fortuitous circumstances rather than of effective juridical control (Scarr 1967: 124).

The view we have from this letter is markedly different from many of the texts Becke was to write celebrating British colonization as far more successful and benevolent than its German counterpart. His stated disaffection for British citizenship and disdain for British law in the Pacific did not prevent Becke from applying in 1893 to the Western Pacific High Commission to become resident commissioner of the Gilbert and Ellice Islands.

If the interference of the Royal Navy, under the aegis of the Western Pacific High Commission, is seen as a hindrance to commercial success for the trader, so is the influence of missionaries. The missionary intervention upsets the balance of the trading relationship, a balance that Becke prefers should be firmly in his favor. Again there is nostalgia for times past when the Pacific islanders were easy prey to the beachcombers, castaways, and traders living beyond the administrative governance of the European powers or the moral governance of missionaries. In much the same way as latter-day anthropologists search for cultures to study that are uncorrupted by contact with Western culture, Becke seeks Pacific islanders uncorrupted—in their "natural state"—not for study, but for exploitation.

Becke's attitude to the missionary enterprise, however, is as ambiguous as his relationship to British colonialism. At various times he praises the missionary endeavor and at others condemns it. In a much later article on the cession of British rights in Samoa to Germany at the turn of the century, he concludes that the missionary enterprise in Samoa will be badly affected by severance from the "nation to which they owe their enlightenment, their schools, their churches, and the guidance of their esteemed missionaries" (1899–1900: 220). Wherever the red ensign of England is seen waving amid the swaying coco-palms of the Gilbert and Ellice Islands, he writes,

> you will everywhere see the beneficial results which have accrued to the natives from the intercourse and training they have received from teachers educated at the great training institution at [Samoa] . . . From Samoa these young men and women have radiated in all directions among the groups of the South, and (latterly) the Western, Pacific . . . they live and do excellent work among the low-lying atolls of the Equatorial Pacific . . . The native teacher, however, has his faults, and needs supervision by his white superiors, in the absence of which he too often becomes tyrannical, disposed to take the bit between his teeth and cause dissension between his flock and the white traders, by his desire to show his authority. (220)

Toward the end of this passage Becke tempers his outright enthusiasm for the missionary enterprise and alludes to the "native" teachers being too zealous, a comment that could be read in the light of his own disputes with missionaries over trading. Whether the criticism of his letter is directed at his Samoan missionary friend or not is unclear, although as he exchanges food with "the missionary and his wife" it seems unlikely. His reference to cunning and avariciousness seems to suggest that the balance of the trading relationship has tipped toward the Nanumangans rather than himself. Whatever the case, there is a rather large gap between seeing missionization as the curse of the islands to praising its beneficial results.

Nanumaga
Aug 24. 1880

My dear mama

So many important (to me) events have happened since last writing 8th July that I have had no time to continue my letter, first of all we have been to Nanumea the natives made a signal fire about a month and on the following night all the people and I gathered on the beach to see if the Nanumea people would answer our signal, we waited till midnight and I was about to turn in when a prolonged shout made me turn back and we saw all the sky to the westward in a fiery glow, it died away in about a minute and then came again - so then we knew that the Nanumeans were expecting us - next day at sunrise we started in five canoes the one I was in containing Ioane, Eline his wife two other men and the King of Nanumaga, we had a fine breeze from the S.E and in two hours were out of sight of land in the open ocean. We sailed on all day till dark when one of our canoes capsized we then took down sails and waited for the fire as we did not see any land and were afraid to run past it in the dark. We saw the Nanumaga fires every hour but none from where we thought Nanumea to be, at ten oclock a heavy squall set in with a wild sea and cold rain two men constantly bailing to keep us from foundering, poor Eline was wet through till Ioane and I made a covering of the sail and I gave her a change of my clothes, the natives now commenced to get frightened and wanted to turn back but Ioane and Eline and I held out, at midnight it cleared up and then Eline called to me to look and we saw a glorious blaze from Nanumea about 20 miles away - we set sail and passed over the reef at 4. am.

Here to my astonishment I found two white men traders Alfred and a man named Harry Johnson a very decent young fellow, who took me to his house, he is married to a native girl and is doing very well. We intended only to remain 4 days at Nanumea but our people quarrelled with the Nanumeans who seized our canoes and trouble was brewing but after 16 days delay we got away again and after a bad passage back we reached our own island in safety. I forgot to say though that only two canoes came back one small and mine, the other three were too frightened. I brought back three cats with me which I got from Pepa, Harry's wife.

On the day after our return I had a big meeting of the people and I am glad to say that matters are all right again, I have opened my trade again, they have agreed to my demands and as everything was just as merry as marriage bells I got ready a party to go with me to the Grand Local Reef to catch sharks for the sake of their fins we were all ready to go last Monday, food cooked etc and just as I was leaving the house two children came running along out of breath to say that they had seen a "Vaka Motu" (Big Ship) coming round the other side of the island and ten minutes afterwards you can imagine how delighted I was to see the old "The Venus" - to give you an idea of how the natives like me, as soon as they saw the "Venus" all the native girls came down to my house each with a new mat in their hands and some with brooms to clean the house and make it look nice when the Captain came on shore and as these mats are each worth a dollar 30 mats was no mean present, when the Captain, Supercargo and I came on shore I found the house scrupulously clean and all the rooms covered with handsome sleeping mats, not a bit of rubbish any where and a large amount of green cocoanuts ready for us to drink. my copra greatly disappointed me only turning out 3300 lbs. I expected there would be 6000. However Captain Cummings was so pleased with me and my house that he said he would not fail to give a good a/c of me to A. T. De W. My friend Senior I was glad to see again but he could not come ashore. At sundown The "Venus" stood away to the S.S.E for Nukufetau taking 200 passengers from here to Nukufetau to remain there a week so I expect her back in ten days - there are now only about 10 men and 30 women on the island with me - my little Pautoe has gone too - her parents went and I did not like to keep her. Ioane and Eline have also gone. I want you to tell Alfred that Mr MacKenzie supercargo of "The Venus" told me that it may happen that De Wolf will close up his island businesses and so I am writing to him to ask him to let me stay on here and I will pay him for his trade in two years time and carry on the business myself - I am pretty confident he will trust me, in that case I will like Alfred to come here with me as we will do well. I will hear from De W. in 5 months and will then write to Alfred to tell him what is the result.

I must now say good bye. I will give this letter to Senior. if he comes to see you I hope you will make him welcome for my sake. With love to all. dear Mama

Your affectionately Louie

Commentary

After describing the use of signal fires for navigation and his intention to travel to Nanumea, this third letter gives an account of the journey. Despite his mention of the capsizing of a canoe and being hit by a squall, this letter minimizes the dangerous nature of the journey. Some of the Nanumangans want to turn back, but rather than considering that their reasons may be sound, Becke constructs them as "frightened." The extent of the danger is revealed in one of his stories, which describes a tragedy that occurred on that same route a number of years earlier. "The Rangers of Tia Kau" describes a journey that went dreadfully wrong when a party were taken by sharks when their canoes were hit by a squall near the shark-infested reef of Tia Kau in 1872. Of a party of seventy men, women, and children, only two men survived. Becke probably moderates the danger of the journey so as not to alarm his mother. However, in doing so he writes himself as the fearless masculine adventurer, revealing the extent to which Becke fashions himself as a courageous man who transcends the mundane in taking risks.

This letter, too, conveys the ups and downs of the trader's life. Again there is optimism derived from the resolution of the conflict with the Nanumangans in terms favorable to Becke and the reopening of the trade store; at the same time, there is the disappointment of not having nearly as much copra as he had thought. The captain of the ship promises to give a good report of the trading station to Tom De Wolf. It is characteristic of Becke that, despite the ominous news that De Wolf is likely to abandon the business, he remains optimistic, suggesting to Alfred that he come to the islands and that both of them "will do well."

Like many of the trading firms that operated in the Pacific in the nineteenth century, De Wolf and Company did close down, withdrawing from the region with losses of £20,000, according to Becke (1895a: 287). Because of his inexperience in this type of trade, unlike his larger rivals in the islands, De Wolf made many mistakes which, as Munro remarks, "resulted in costly failures and setbacks" (1980: 32). The main problem identified by Munro is that De Wolf failed to consolidate his trade in one region before extending it beyond that place. Whereas the larger firms had been working at building their trading empires for twenty or so years, he tried to establish one virtually overnight. With his network spread so wide, he was unable to service the trading stations adequately with the shipping he had available (32).[3] For Becke, the collapse of De Wolf was due to the "extraordinary" manner in which he required his traders to carry out business. In an interview several years after Becke had left the islands, he remarked: "This firm then carried out business on—to commercial ideas—most extraordinary lines. They started off with the idea of dealing fairly and squarely with white trader and native alike. The result was a most disastrous failure. We (the firm's *employes* [sic]) all had most stringent instructions as to our line of conduct. We were not to intermeddle in native politics, not to sell grog, not to contract an indefinite number of marriages, and, above all, to pay fairly for all native produce" (1895a: 287).[4]

Whether Becke or De Wolf's other traders conformed to these ideals is unclear.[5] Certainly in his later writings, as we have suggested, Becke tends to fashion himself as a colonist with character who followed the behavioral precepts of his employer. Implicit in the quotation from Becke above is a criticism of De Wolf's "extraordinary" way of doing business. Clearly Becke believes that fair trading is not the way to run a successful business. Fortunately for Becke, Tom De Wolf was generous in giving him some thousands of pounds of trade goods at a time when the firm was failing badly.

August 28. 1880

My dear Mama

"The Venus" not yet back - dead calmed for a whole week. however I expect her to-morrow on Monday; on Friday the "Vaitupule-mele" came here Willie Williams sent her to me for his copra which I delivered. I got it all off by sundown. I had bought a cash box from the captain and came on shore and had agreed with him to come off in the morning just as I got on shore at dark a wild squall came on and the schooner signalled she was off, but I ran to the house got some money but missed the canoe, but I swam over the reef and the schooner ran in and picked me up. I can tell you I enjoyed a glass of grog when I got on board. I came ashore at 9 p.m and "Vaitupulemele" left for Nukufetau.

[unsigned]

Island of Nanumaga
Sunday August 28. 1880

My dear Mama

At daylight I was called by my cook who said a ship was in sight I ran down to the beach expecting to see "The Venus" but it is the native vessell "Vaitupulemele" lying becalmed about 10 miles off; she left here last Friday and must have got away about 70 miles when it fell calm and she has drifted back here.

I hope she will drift in closer today as I want to try and get a boat compass from her. I forgot to tell you that I am a great pig man now I have 22 pigs in my styes and two days ago Mrs Pig increased my stock by twins, it takes just 50 cocoanuts a day to feed them; I sold 6 to "The Venus" if Mr Senior should come to [pass?] to see you and he says he is coming back here please ask Edwin to try and get him two dogs for me, a male and female any breed, and Senior will bring them to me. To day being Sunday I am alone in the house my cook and housemaid have gone to church and - servants wages are not very high here my cook Ume $1.50 per month and Tafeta housemaid $1.75 per month. I forgot to say that I had a visitor here in the "Vaitupulemele" a trader from an adjacent island Nuitas [Niutao] Geo Winchcombe - four years on Nuitas and cannot yet talk the language in fact I had to interpret for him. such a man to talk, my ears are actually tingling now, I don't know how much more I would have suffered if it had not been for a case of gin I produced and by liquoring him up freely I got a little respite. he is a fair sample of too many island traders fond of liquor and never happy without some grievance to relate against the natives, these are the men that give the missionaries such a pull over *all* traders - they are no better than the natives - they let their children run about wild and devote all their energies to the gin-bottle, but still at this present time the general islander trader is as a rule a respectable and fairly educated man, there are few left of the old class, the dissolute whaler or escaped convict.

It is a lovely calm day today the sea smooth as glass; before [?] 11 oclock I am going to walk over to the windward side of the island to see if I can see "The Venus" coming back this is such a little island that it is only 20 minutes walk *across* the island. although it is 4 miles long but very narrow; last night I baked 4 loaves and left three in a box and while I was asleep a pig came in and eat three but very considerately left me one for Sunday; (this is no doubt the result of missionary teaching)[?] I think Olive would like to see my two cats and a pet pig I have, they always sleep together piggy lies down and the cats sprawl across him like wet dish-cloths. I had a tame pigeon here and kept him in a box and the black cat was for ever glaring at him with hungry eyes - on day she got into the box while I was away I drove her out and the pigeon came out too but it was *inside* of the cat. - I expect "John Williams" here next month and then I hope to get a letter from you telling me you are all well at home. About 3 weeks ago while I was at St. Augustine's Island the natives saw a large ship painted white passing to the N.W; it must have been the "San Francisco" one of Goddeffroys vessells going to the Carolines. Generally on this island only one vessell is seen in a year. I wish a man-of-war would come so as to make a little money; and to get some books or newspapers from her. It is very probable that I may leave here soon (but to return) to proceed to the Marshall Islands on business that I have neglected too long and of vital importance to me. If ever you get any papers to send me please do so - they will require 1d postage - but send to C/o Hamilton else the postoffice at Apia will claim them. any papers or books will be acceptable. Hamiltons agent in Sydney is *John Williams* of Apia 51 Pitt St. but I hear he is a regular nipper - so don't send a parcel if he wants to charge you freight. Will you tell Alfred that if he comes to Sydney to call on the agents of Henderson & Macfarlane of Auckland who now do all the business down here and if he chooses they will I daresay give him an agency if he desires to come to the islands again, I do not know who their agents are but it is easy to find out by enquiring from such as Rabone Fagoto or other people who do business with the islands - else he could write to Mr Henderson of H & M. Merchants, Auckland who is a very nice young fellow I hear - they have five vessells in the trade and stations in both the North and South Pacific and pay their agents salary besides a commission, the salary is $50.00 per month. Their agents here are Flower on Funafuti - Thompson on Nuie [Niue] - Johnson on Nanomea [Nanumea] and many others who I do not know - they are a very respectable firm. Tell Alfred that if I cannot arrange with De Wolf in the event of his closing up to keep me on I intend to go in with Henderson and Macfarlane.

With fond love to all at home
Yours affectionately
Louis G. Becke

Venus arrived sails tonight I send this by Mr Senior.

Commentary

A substantial proportion of this interrupted letter is concerned with the various comings and goings of ships and with domestic arrangements. It is most illuminating, however, for its account of the visit of another trader, George Winchcombe, because it prefigures a theme that becomes dominant in Becke's Pacific tales, the theme of "going native."

From Becke's account it is obvious that the two men did not get on well together. Whatever the cause of Becke's dislike, his comments show that he is fashioning himself as superior to Winchcombe, as a trader of character who has not fallen. Far from Winchcombe's being described as decent, like the traders Becke met on the visit to Nanumea recounted in the earlier letter of August 24, 1880, he is described as intemperate and disagreeable. In writing that Winchcombe is "no better than the natives," Becke is suggesting that he has descended to the level of the local people—he has "gone native." Although earlier he nostalgically praised the past era when traders were allowed to carry on their business free of government intervention, Becke now disparages past traders as dissolute whalers or escaped convicts, disreputable and uneducated.

As we have already noted, Winchcombe appears under the thinly disguised name of Winchcombly in the story "Tarria, the Swimmer," published many years after this letter was written. Set mainly on the islands of Nanumea and Nanumanga, it tells of a degenerate white trader, Winchcombly, who has a disagreement with a trader from Nanumanga, Watson, an alter ego of Becke, and eventually tries to kill him. A third character in this story is a Man Friday–like Tokelan black man from Onotoa, who selflessly gives up his life to save Watson's. As in the Becke letter, Winchcombly is presented as an intemperate and disagreeable character, "a drink-besotted, unclean, creature, illiterate and violent-tempered" (1923: 99). Not only is he constructed in this narrative as a generally obnoxious person but also as a racist. At their first meeting a quarrel arose because Winchcombly did not think Watson should be staying in the same house as a black man, suggesting that to do so makes the blacks disrespectful of whites. " 'A nice sorter white man you are to put up with a ———— Kanaka missionary when there's a white man liv'n' here. It's the likes o'you as makes these rotten natives so damned saucy to white men' " (99–100). In the ensuing quarrel, Watson questions whether Winchcombly is a white man, suggesting that the dirty, unkempt, and barefoot Winchcombly may call himself a white man, but Watson does not. He concludes by saying that if he had a wash he might resemble one. It is paradoxical that Watson has recourse to the language of race to impugn the racist Winchcombly. This clearly demonstrates that Becke's discourses of the degenerate white are embedded in wider racial narratives that encompass both black and white.

Nanumaga. Ellice Group S. Pacific
February 21. 1881.

My dear Mama. I have had a rough time of it since last writing - on the 2^{d.} of this month my station was destroyed by a hurricane. For some two or three days previous to this we knew that something strange was to happen, many strange sea-birds unknown to the natives came flying from the westward and with strange cries settled on the beach and on the cocoanut trees, for nearly two months past it had been blowing heavily from the westward, but on the 1st the wind fell and the sea made a curious noise like the bellowing of some beast. Next day it commenced to blow and and my anxiety was great but lest the house would give way, although it withstood the force of the wind it succumbed to a new and unexpected danger. At three oclock in the morning it then being pitch dark and raining and blowing furiously, and dead low water I was sitting in one of my servants houses with three natives of De Peyster's island and some of my workpeople watching my dwelling house was in danger from two tall cocoa nut trees which every moment threatened to fall and crush in the roof. It was now blowing furiously the air filled with salt spray and as I expected a change at turn of tide I sent a little girl to crawl along on the sand to the beach and see if the tide was coming in - in a few minutes she came flying back saying. "The sea has gone away, there is nothing but tarevereve" (great empty space). Anticipating something serious we ran into the big house and the next minutes with a strange roaring sound the sea rose up like a wall and dashed over the reef in one mighty wave and swept up into the village, sweeping away fifteen houses like chaff - the next wave dashed into my front room and filled it with coral rocks and sand. How glad I am to say that by working like demons we saved all the trade, or at all events almost everything of value, by the time I had got everything carried into the rear of the village and out of danger the wind was at its height and the sound it made was like the droning of countless flocks of bees, and sea after sea rolled up into the village, in a few minutes my house, trade house, copra houses, fowl houses, pig houses etc were things that had been, and were piled up without much regard to regularity in a heap, together with sundry drowned pigs and other live stock, the next wave they went away to sea together with a few native houses. I lost some copra but saved 7000 lbs and also saved my canoe which is a valuable one, so altogether I won't grumble; as I might have lost all.

I have written to De W. to tell him of this - I estimate general loss at $250:00 to $300:00. The natives say it is 35 years since such a storm as this visited the island. It is now the 21st and you will perhaps be surprised to know that I am back again in the old position with new house, copra houses, cook houses, and man servants and maid servants and all things that are his. Some hundreds of thousands of young cocoanuts have been destroyed and I am anxiously awaiting the arrival of one of our vessells, to consult as to what is to be done. My vessell is now some five months overdue - I will now say good bye and with love to all I am dear Mama. Your affectionate Son. Louis.

Commentary

In Becke's marvelously vivid description of the impending disaster of the hurricane, we catch a glimpse of the writer he was to become. Like much of his later fictional writings, this letter has a rawness and intensity that conveys the reader in imagination to the tiny Pacific island to be confronted by ominous signs of overwhelming disaster.

This letter again reflects the fluctuations in fortune of Becke's trading venture. Although disaster strikes in the form of a hurricane and accompanying tidal wave, ruin is (at least temporarily) averted. Despite the destruction and flooding of his house, Becke sustains a comparatively small loss, and he rebuilds his trading station, which rises phoenix-like from the ruin. Despite the disruption, Becke still conveys some of the optimism that characterizes his earlier letters. He doesn't want to grumble at his losses, as they could have been worse. Again, although he may be avoiding alarming his mother about the dangers of living in the Equatorial Pacific, he is also presenting himself as a man who overcomes adversity and disaster.

In writing of these events, Becke makes his own self central. This is mainly a narrative of Becke's endeavors to take charge in the face of disaster. Apart from a slight mention of the effects of the hurricane on the Nanumangans, their presence is largely discounted. When they appear they are unnamed, as small players on the stage where Becke has the main role. Understandable as this may seem, given the nature of his audience, this foregrounding also has a broader effect. Like the account of the canoe journey discussed above, this is an example of Becke writing himself as the masculine colonial adventurer. By taking disaster and danger in his stride, and indeed seeking them out, Becke is fashioning himself in a particular way: as a man with pluck.

Although Becke rebuilds after the disaster, some of the early optimism of this letter is dissipated at its conclusion when he mentions the extent of destruction of the coconut plantation and anxiously awaits one of De Wolf's vessels which is five months late, a lateness that reflects the crumbling state of the De Wolf trading network, and ultimately Becke's role in it.

Schooner "Redcoat"
Island of Nukufetau.
Ellice Group
May 1. 1881

My dear Alfred

This is to tell you that the "Redcoat" arrived at Nanumaga and brought me a letter from you and an illustrated news, I also received two papers from you by a New Zealand vessell. Mr De W wrote me a very nice letter & said that the captain of the Redcoat was instructed to close up the business and that in my favour only he made an exception and the Captain has given me Two Thousand dollars in trade and I have only given him my note of hand to pay as I can to any other firm whom he may appoint and he (De W) said most likely he would get Henderson & McFarlane to call for my copra. This of course is a good offer for me and so I left Nanumaga to come here and will wait here for one of Hendersons vessells to call here and take me up to the Carolines. I have seen Mr Henderson himself some two months ago and told him that I would like to get a station from him and he told me that if the Redcoat called and squared up with me he would give me a station in the Carolines - so I have come to live on this island until Hendersons send a vessell for me. I expect to remain here for about five months. I will write to you again by the earliest opportunity and tell you where I am going as perhaps I may not engage with Henderson at all.

Address as usual to Hamilton I am so busy landing my stores and getting a few lessons in navigation that I have no time to write more. if this should reach you in Sydney be sure to call on the Redcoat and see Capt Foster. I have given him a letter to Aubrey. - he is a fine young fellow.

In haste
Yours Louis

Unlike the other letters, this is written to Becke's brother Alfred, and shows that he has moved from Nanumanga to the island of Nukufetau, about two hundred miles to the southeast. From this letter we see that the demise of De Wolf and Company that had been presaged in the earlier letters has finally occurred, although the effect of this collapse on Becke has been minimized considerably by Tom De Wolf's generosity. The stop on Nukufetau is a temporary one, being for the purpose of waiting for a trading vessel of the firm of Henderson and Macfarlane, the company Becke hopes to work for.

Like Becke's previous employer, Henderson and Macfarlane was a small trading firm, but with a long history of commercial enterprise on the colonial periphery. As one laudatory account puts it, this firm "was to blazen many a splendid chapter in New Zealand's history, from the famous '49 goldrush to the Yukon through the Maori Wars, to the stirring adventurous days of the Pacific traders" (Hallett n.d.: 1). Despite its long history of trading elsewhere, its entry into trading in the Pacific was relatively recent at the time that Becke worked for them, the company establishing itself at Suwarrow in 1875 (Hallett n.d.: 25). According to Hallett, this was a period when the South Seas "was a 'No Man's Land'—a magnetic attraction for the adventurers of the world where trade, adventure, easy-living, large profits and no law made it appear a paradise" (25). Whether in fact the large profits were realized is doubtful, and Henderson and Macfarlane, like many a trading firm, were not very successful and their traders even less so.

As indicated in the next letter, dated September 24, 1881, Becke wrote to his mother while on Nukufetau about some "extraordinary adventures" he had there, but unfortunately that letter was lost. It was on the island of Nukufetau that Becke married a local woman, Nelea Tikena (Day 1967: 35, 150 n.16). As Becke never mentions in his later interviews or writings that he was married there, it is doubtful that he would have told his mother. This silence is consistent with the way that he uses silences and absences generally in his writings to fashion himself as a colonist who, through reserve and propriety, maintains his "civilized" difference from the locals. Some insight into Becke's residence on Nukufetau can be gained from other sources, however. One such account comes from the trader George Winchcombe, of whom Becke had written so disparagingly.

In a section of notes under the heading "Beck[e] Traders and Goods Landed in Teachers Home," Winchcombe writes:

An Englishman Lewis Beck[e] arrived here May 7. 1881 in the Sch "Redcoat" to await the arrival of another Vessel to take him to the line Islands.

The Natives were not at all anxious about his landing here, from some previous tidings of him about the Islands & offered him accommodation, he therefore went to Teacher's house and soon made arrangements to land here & and live with the Teacher "[Mekish]." accompanied him to the Vessel, his trade and other [goods] landed & placed in missionary home, he also [went] and slept there himself.

Among other things were about 50 Gun with ample Ammunition & an about 30 Cases Liquor, here he remained [several weeks] passing his time by firing gun, day after day greatly disturbing the quiet [life] of the Island, we visited each other occasionally & and I purchased few Articles of him in the Teachers home & drank grog there with him.

There was a little girl remaining at Teacher's house as playmate to his little girl, she might have been about 14 years old, Beck was middle aged man—and as I can suppose, influenced by Effects of drink, he prepared this little girl to give her consent to marry him, then freely presenting the Father with cloth & other things won his approval & willing[ness] to the marriage, but it was con[jectured] by the people, that the Teacher would not marry a child at that age & contented themselves i[t] [could] therefore not be carried into Effect, they were however pretty disappointed for when the appointed day arrived, the marriage was solemnized by the Teacher in the Church.

May 14 1881. "Emerald" ship of War arrived, Captn. Maxwell & and some of the officers landed and as the Captn. said he wished to see the Missionary Buildings, myself & Beck conducted him to the Teacher's House, [then] to the Church & School. While in the Teacher's house, the Captn. remarked to Beck, that he was well supplied with fire arms & Liquor & enquired if it was for sale on the Islands & Beck replied in the negative.

Aug. 14 1881. Beck left the Island in the Schn. "Orwell" for the Line & returned his young wife to the Father again, since which she has been fined 2 or 3 times for Criminal offences. Said he would return to his wife in 1 or 2 years.

A few weeks prior to Becks departure, he quarrelled with the Teacher about something, & posted papers on the trees about the Church, on a Saturday night, charging him the teacher with being a liar &c, this was written in Samoan language and remained up all day Sunday. This is what Beck & the Native told me. I did not read them myself.[6]

The veracity of Winchcombe's account of Becke, like Becke's account of him, can be questioned. The two men clearly did not like each other, and each constructs the other in a particular way. Whatever the personal motives behind his account, Winchcombe selects those aspects of his rival's behavior that would be disapproved of in certain circles and that could be used against Becke. For example, Winchcombe writes disapprovingly of Becke's living with the local teacher, not maintaining the reserve and distance that should characterize the relations between races. Winchcombe represents Becke as idle, immoral, and dissolute, a disagreeable, argumentative man, a heavy drinker, and of questionable morality in his relations with women. Becke, it seems, has taken his marriage lightly, using and abandoning a very young woman, leaving her ruined. Like Becke's portrayal of him, Winchcombe portrays Becke as a degenerate white, who forsakes the norms and behaviors of civilized white society.

Island of Peru [Beru], Kingsmill Group
Sept 24. 1881
S. Lat 1.20 E. Lon 176.21

My dear Mama. I am sorry that I have nothing but bad, bad news for you as regards myself for we were castaway on this island on the 24th of August last and I lost all I possessed in the world. After my last letters to you from Nukufetau by the "Redcoat" I remained on Nukufetau waiting for Henderson Macfarlane's vessell. H.M.S. Emerald came and bought me over 30 papers and two letters from you, one from Aubrey, one from Hamilton, one of your letters *was only a month old*. The "Emerald" left next day, the Captain and officers were very kind to me and supplied me with provisions, I am sorry I could not write by her as the Capt Maxwell said he would be in Sydney by the 25th of July, but as I had some land disputes to settle I had no time to write. At last on Aug 6th. the long expected vessell came for me from Auckland the "Orwell" and the supercargo Flower had instructions to take me to Apiang [Abaiang] in this group and I was to form a head station there and to be manager for the firm of all their business in the Kingsmill and Marshall Groups. I packed up and we sailed next day and after touching at various islands we made this island on Aug 24th and at 11. a.m. at night we lost the vessell and with difficulty saved our lives. I have written to Aubrey an account of the wreck and have asked him to forward it on to you so that you may read it and then send on to Alfred. The natives plundered and pillaged the vessell, we were without arms and I had the maddening sensation of seeing myself robbed and dared not raise my hand else we would have all lost our lives. The firm (H & M) have an agency here and we all went to live in the traders house a very nice fellow a Tyrolese named Francisco Vollino. We set to work to save some provisions but the natives robbed us almost as fast as we got it, however we saved some at this time all my worldly goods was a piece of red silk I had wrapped round my loins, afterwards though I got a good many thin clothes, but unfortunately the climate here is such that I never go beyond wearing a pair of cotton trousers. The day after the wreck the Captain called us together and asked for volunteers to go in one of the boats saved from the wreck to the island of Apamama [Abemama] distant 300 miles, the crew refused, the mate, I and two others volunteered, but as luck would have it next day a barque called the "George Noble" belonging to a Chinese firm in Sydney came here and Capt Evers took Capt Robinson, five men and a boat on board and was to take them as near to Apamama as he could and then they were to pull. At sunset the "Geo Noble" left and so far that is all we know of our Captain and crew. He (Our Captain) was to go to Apamama and try and charter a schooner named the "Coronet" belonging to the King of Apamama to come here and take us all up to Auckland. If the Coronet was not there he said he would wait there till one of our vessells named the "Belle Brandon" came there from the Marshalls and as young Mr Henderson is on board of her she would come up here at once and take us away. We are daily expecting a vessell either the "Coronet" or the "Belle Brandon," but perhaps the "George Noble" will come here first on her way up to Sydney if so you will soon see me as [well?] Le Brun the mate, Boatswain and I will come up to Sydney in her if the Captain will give us a passage. I am now quite dependent on H & M and I hope the "Orwells" loss will not hurt them much; but it will be some months before they have another vessel ready to take her place and if I remain here with the Supercargo and wait till we go up to Auckland I will when I get there be a stranger in a strange place and no money to keep me, but if I get to Sydney I know some people I think whom I can stay with till I get orders to report myself at Auckland to H & M; and there is always a steamer every week. In case however we cannot get to Sydney in the "Geo Noble" you must always in future direct your letters to me care of Henderson & Macfarlane, Merchants, Auckland and if I am in Auckland I will of course get them, if not they will keep them for me, for the firm in Auckland I suppose do not know anything of me as I was engaged by young Mr Henderson who is now down in the Marshall Group and it was by his orders that the "Orwell" came to Nukufetau for me. I must tell you that when I left Nukufetau I had two splendid collections of shells one for you and one for Aubrey; they are all at the bottom of the sea now. I also got another letter from you by the "Orwell" and 16 papers making 4 letters and 46 papers within this last 3 months, so I am sure none of your letters to me have miscarried and I had written you a letter of 20 pages telling you of some very extraordinary adventures that happened to me in Nukufetau in consequence of the visit of the "Emerald" I had also letters prepared for Edwin, Alfred & Aubrey, they were of course all lost when we were wrecked. I had them all packed in that little box I made from the wreck of the "Leonora" when we were castaway on Strongs island in 1875, so that box is gone too. I got it from Fanny when I left Sydney in the "Venus." All the last papers I had from you I never ever opened as I was keeping them till I got settled down at Apiang. In the same box I had $900:00 in English gold, all lost, but a great deal of it found by the natives who won't give it up, and as they are 2000 strong here and we are only 9 all told I will never see that money again. An American Captain who took a great liking to me gave me a gold chronometer watch quite new which he paid [£]40.0.0 for, that I also lost, together with goods to the value of Three thousand dollars - a hard knock for me this time. We were likely at first to have lost all our lives by the natives, but the Captain's conduct was cool & quiet, and fortunately for us all I found a native who could talk Samoan and although we had one fight on the second day there was no bloodshed, till a native picked up one of my rifles on the beach and as the beach was also covered with liquor he also got drunk and shot his own brother dead on the spot in his drunken fury. With the aid of the two Samoan missionaries on the island we have recovered a good deal of the stuff that was stolen by the natives, but all of it that belonged to me was some clothes and 16 Enfield rifles and one revolver. We are expecting the "George Noble" here next week and if I do not get a passage by her I can at least send you a letter. I forgot to tell you that the shells I sent you by Mr Senior were "collared" by Mr De Wolf who sent them to England. When you write to Auckland let me know if you received any letters by the "Redcoat." There is another thing I want to get to Sydney for, for some time I have been suffering from a poisoned foot and the doctor of the man-of-war could do nothing for it on board but said that it can be cured with ice baths, it is very painful and I have now

been bad with it five months, otherwise I am in good health, don't
forget to write to Auckland care of H & M if I don't come up in the
"Geo Noble" to Sydney and with sincere love to all at home I am
dear Mama your affectionate Son Louis G. Becke.

Commentary

Becke's situation has deteriorated badly. After having his trading station
destroyed by a hurricane and his employer's firm collapse, Becke is now
shipwrecked and has lost everything. Emphasizing the enormity of his disaster, he repeats "bad, bad news," and later remarks that it has been a "hard
knock" for him. Unfortunately, a much fuller description of the wrecking
of the ship in another letter appears to have been lost. Partial accounts are
given in some of his later writings, such as the following, drawn from one of
his journalistic accounts of fishing in the Pacific:

> In 1882 I took passage from the Island of Nukufetau in the Ellice Group
> for the Caroline Islands. The vessel was a fine brigantine of 160 tons,
> and was named the *Orwell*. She was, unfortunately, commanded by an
> incompetent, obstinate, self-willed man, who, though a good seaman,
> had no meteorological knowledge and succeeded in losing the ship,
> when lying at anchor, on Peru [Beru] Island, in the Gilbert Group, ten
> days after leaving Nukufetau, simply through disregarding the local
> trader's advice to put to sea. Disastrous as was the incident to me, for
> I lost trade goods and personal effects to the value of over a thousand
> pounds, and came ashore with what I stood in—to wit, a pyjama suit—
> and a bag of Chili dollars . . . (1901a: 155–56)

Some of the detail in this account is different from that in his letter to his
mother, such as the amount of trade goods and clothing he was left with.
Also absent is mention of the losses having been incurred at the hands of
the islanders. These silences downplay the extent of Becke's losses, making
him something other than the bad colonist he is. Through silences and absences Becke rewrites the incident to present himself not as the victim of
islanders, but as stoically taking personal losses in his stride. The original
letter, of course, was written at a time when Becke's anger and emotions
were heightened. Given that he had probably barely escaped with his life
and had lost everything he owned, the revelation of his anger at this moment is understandable, as is the more dispassionate tone he adopted later.

Then, with true imperialist pluck, he is able to put disaster behind him and to make the best of the incident. Afterwards he could congratulate himself from a "fisherman's point of view," having spent most of his three months on the island pursuing one of his passions: fishing (1901a: 156).

Also absent in the later account is the underlying inclination to violence; Becke shows in this letter that he is willing to use it to defend his interests. As with the letter of July 8, where he reports his conflict with the Nanumangans and nostalgically wishes for a return of an earlier period of unencumbered free trade, the threat of recourse to violence underlies his words. This is erased in his later accounts, where he fashions himself as the good colonist who always treats the islanders honorably.

The story "The Brothers-in-Law: A Tale of the Equatorial Islands" provides further insight into his view of the Beru Islanders. The islanders are described as "wild, intractable, and savage people" (1901a: 286), comparable to the degenerate whites there "who spent their days in idleness, drunkenness, and debauchery" (287). Of course, if the Gilbert Islanders are indeed as "wild and intractable" as his letter and later accounts convey, the question arises as to how the resident trader has managed to stay in business or even to stay alive. As Macdonald (1982: 23) has suggested, rather than being inclined to pillage and plunder, the islanders were merely exercising their claim to wreck salvage, a practice established for many years. Successful white residence on the island of Beru was contingent upon abiding by the ways of the islanders. "When Europeans accepted Gilbertese customs and value," as Macdonald has remarked, "there was seldom any difficulty" (23).

> On board the "George Noble"
> Island of Tarawa, Kingsmill Group
> North Lat. 1.50. East Lon 173.00
> [14th Dec. 1881]

dear Mama.

I am coming up to Sydney in the "George Noble," we left Peru on 6th Oct and went to Drummonds Island [Tabiteuea] and there we met the releiving vessell the "Coronet" belonging to the King of Apamama. Capt Robinson on board, going to Peru to take us all up to Auckland Captain Robinson came on board this vessell and made arrangements with me to go on to Sydney and report the "Orwells" affair to the Commodore in Sydney and try and get a man-of-war down - very likely I may have to leave Sydney soon in a man-of-war but of course I cannot tell yet - you will see the arrival of this vessell in the papers and I will telegraph to you as soon as I arrive in Sydney. We are now at Tarawa - natives fighting, and leave tomorrow for Apiang, then to Makin and then direct to Sydney.

December 14. We are now off New Caledonia and as we may meet the Sydney mail steamer I will send this on by her, we are right in her track and if we should meet her she will of course reach Sydney before us; we are now only 900 miles from Sydney heads. I am anxious to get there as my foot is very bad every now and then.

> [unsigned]

Majura [Majuro] (Island of)
Marshall Group
North Pacific
Nov 1. 1882

My dear Mother

I wrote you from Jaluit in this group to tell you where I was etc and sent the letter via California - since then I have been by a curious coincidence sent by by Hernsheim & Co to trade on this island in opposition to Henderson and Macfarlane - it is very unpleasant and distasteful to me in one way as you know I told you that I was under engagement to H & M when the Orwell was lost; and was waiting in Sydney till heard from Mr Henderson but his letter reached Sydney the day after I left and you sent it on to New Britain - had I remained in Sydney one day longer and received that letter it would have been vastly to my interest and have saved me all the misery I suffered in New Britain.

However in about a year or so my time will be up with the German firm and I am sure Mr Henderson will give me a station - their head station is here 30 miles up the lagoon - I went up yesterday as I heard a ship was there and found the barque "India" there - Mr Carr - Supercargo handed me two letters one from you and one from Aubrey both 18 months old - they had gone to Nanumaga but the natives there could not give the Captain of "John Williams" my address I suppose, thence to Nanomea or Samoa and by some means came into Mr Carrs hands who was going to send them to Dead letter office. In future you may have no fear of addressing me under cover to Henderson & Macfarlane of Auckland. I have changed my address so often that the letters cannot keep going astray - but all letters will reach me eventually - do not send anything more via New Britain or Jaluit. Henderson & M are in regular communication with Majura being their head station if there are any letters in Samoa I will get them as I will write now to Hamilton

- and tell him to send them here - H & M are now again sending ships to Samoa. I am in hopes again of getting something from the government for the goods plundered from the Orwell - as Mr Carr tells me the island is to be visited by a man-of-war and fined $15.000:00 or £3000. I may get a little out of this. I must now close in haste as I must take this up myself in a canoe to H & M station to put it on board the India. With best love I am dearest mother.

Affectionately Louis Yours.

nearly clear of fever

Commentary

Written after Becke's arrival in the Marshall Islands, this final letter was written almost eleven months after the one of December 1881. Again it conveys Becke's plans to his mother after further changes in his circumstances. He has just spent some time trading in New Britain, which he says caused him "misery." There are no letters surviving from this time, but it appears likely that illness was a factor in this evaluation, as indicated by his remark that he is nearly free of fever.

The change to another island group has meant a change of employer. Becke is now working for the German firm Hernsheim and Company, in competition with his old employers Henderson and Macfarlane. We are told this is "unpleasant and distasteful," perhaps more so than Becke reveals here, for in his writings and interviews he views Germans with disdain, reproducing the imperial rivalry between Germany and Britain.[7] In an interview in the *St. James Gazette* in 1896, Becke speaks of the German colonization of New Guinea as a "howling and dismal failure" (1896b). "The fact is," he says, "the Germans cannot colonize. People in Australia like the German colonist under British rule; but under German rule the German colonist is 'a ghastly failure.'" All the islands in Melanesia, Polynesia, and Micronesia, he complains, were first opened up by the British trader, but many have now been annexed by Germany, driving the British trader out: "It is the special business of the German authorities to drive the British trader out of the very islands which British people opened up." Although to some extent he is reflecting the changes in the colonial map of the Pacific that occurred in the late 1880s, when various parts of the Western and Equatorial Pacific were divided between Britain and Germany in the Anglo-German Agreement of 1886, Becke is mainly reflecting upon the economic dominance of German firms during the time he was a trader.[8] During the period encompassed by these letters, for example, German interests controlled an estimated 70 percent of the commerce in the Pacific basin (Munro 1980: 24). Aside from the German New Guinea Company, whose activities in New Guinea were an economic failure, German firms were more successful than the other firms Becke worked for.[9] The same distaste for German colonialism, but not colonialism more generally, is often evident in Becke's Pacific stories, which feature many degenerate and violent Germans who are usually contemptuously referred to as "Dutchmen."

Despite having to work for a German firm, in this letter Becke is again optimistic—this time about receiving some compensation from the Beru Islanders, as a warship was to be dispatched there. Eventually one of the warships of the Royal Navy's Australian Station, HMS *Espiegle,* was sent to Beru to extract a penalty. After being threatened with a naval bombardment, the islanders agreed to pay a fine of thirty tons of copra, but later bitterly protested the injustice of the fine (Macdonald 1982: 23). Whether, in fact, Becke received any compensation is uncertain.

This is the last surviving letter of Becke's time working as a trader. How long he continued to work in the Marshall Islands and whether he found any success there is unknown. As we suggested previously, it seems probable that he remained in the Pacific until he returned to Australia in 1886. We do know that the success he did find was not as a colonist but as an author recounting tales of life in the Pacific.

In his letters to his mother Becke presents himself as an upright colonist with sufficient character to resist "going native."[1] This theme becomes far more strikingly apparent in his later Pacific tales. Many of these were written in London at the turn of the century, when degeneration and decadence were exciting the popular imagination.[2] As his earlier letters testify, Becke was well aware of the notion that whites living in the Pacific were susceptible to moral and cultural degeneration. At its most rudimentary, degeneration was a counternarrative to the idea that progress was inevitable. Rather than the future's being assuredly bright and promising as progressivist historical narratives postulated, degenerationism held that there was the possibility of decline and regress, that the future also held the potential of being grim. Historically, degeneration has connoted not only cultural decline, but also moral and physical decline. As Pick has remarked, degeneration has been an exceedingly fluid signifier and as such cannot be "reduced to a fixed axiom or theory . . . [rather] it was a shifting term produced, inflected, refined, and reconstituted" (1989: 7).[3] Accordingly, the term has been used in a wide range of social and scientific theory, from medicine to anthropology, from psychology to criminology, and from biology to geography. The idea of degeneration, however, was not restricted to the nineteenth century, nor was it only "a European disorder," as Pick has argued.[4] Rather, it was also a colonial disorder and took on particular saliences in that milieu. Becke's stories of beachcombers, castaways, deserters, traders, and escaped convicts recount the lives of men who transgress the racial and cultural boundaries, falling to become like the colonial other. "In those days," Becke writes, "there were many white men in these islands. Some were traders, some were but *papalagi tafea* [beachcombers] who spent their days in idleness, drunkenness, and debauchery, casting aside all pride and living like these savage people, with but a girdle of grass around their naked waists, their hands ever imbued in the blood of their fellow white men or that of the men of the land" (Becke and Jeffery 1901: 287).

Like Winchcombe, many of the characters in Becke's stories are described as "generally a rough character—a runaway from some Australian or American Whaler, or a wandering Ishmael who, for reasons of his own, preferred living among the intractable, bawling, and poverty-stricken people of the equatorial Pacific" (1894[1955]: 98). At other times, his protagonists are described as "white loafers" or "poor whites." A great number of his stories reflect Becke's own life as a failed colonist, whose only profit was the memories of his time in the Pacific. Becke's stories tell, as he says, "of those restless wanderers who range the Pacific in search of the fortune they always mean to gain, but which never comes to them, except in some few instances" (1902: 175).

From the Marshall Islands in the northwest to the Pitcairn Island in the southeast, the geographic range of Becke's stories is far and wide across the Pacific. A number of stories are located in Australia, recounting his times working or adventuring there.[5] Many are drawn from his experiences in the Equatorial Pacific, and many feature the islands where he was a trader, such as the Gilbert and Ellice Islands.[6] Others feature the island of Majuro in the Marshall Islands, from which one of the letters was written.[7] Unlike his letters, some of these stories are rich in ethnographic detail, particularly when it comes to subsistence activities such as fishing, in which Becke took a particularly active interest. Stories such as "The Fisher Folk of Nukufetau," "A Hundred Fathoms Deep," and "The 'Palu' of the Equatorial Pacific" document some of the fishing techniques of the islands where he traded, as well as Becke's own sporting feats.

The style of Becke's stories is unpretentious, with a rawness and intensity that may be labeled realism or naturalism. He was a masterful storyteller who, though perhaps falling short of the literary merit of, say, Conrad, could produce a gripping story. Although to call him a writer of imperialist adventure fiction is justified, to do so without qualification discounts the complexity of his writings.[8] Likewise, to typify him as a racist and colonist is to overlook the complexity of his views. Both the letters and the Pacific tales display the conflicting interests and tensions within the colonizing cultures. Becke is no simple racist who disparages and denigrates all that is other; his letters give the impression of a man who, despite some conflict, was able to establish a rapport with the islanders with whom he lived.

Ambivalent Images

Like Conrad's, Becke's views of race and colonialism are ambivalent and fluid. He decries certain forms of racism and colonialism and the excesses of some colonists, but not all. For both Conrad and Becke, British imperialism with its civilizing mission was acceptable, and even praised by Becke, whereas other European imperial ventures, such as the Belgian (Conrad) and the German (Becke) are condemned. In a number of interviews and articles Becke decries the German colonization of New Guinea, which he says has had "disastrous results," but praises the British colonization there, which he says has been accompanied "with the steady march of progress and civilisation."[9] As noted earlier, many of his stories feature the brutal German, whose violence and "savagery" make him more akin to the "natives."[10]

Despite his generally enthusiastic support of some colonialism, particularly the British variety, the Pacific tales do not unequivocally celebrate the imperial venture, as do some texts in the adventure tradition. Many of his stories speak of the brutality of a settler and imperial culture that is ruthless in the pursuit of economic expansion and profit. They capture with stark realism the greed, corruption, and violence that has accompanied the colonization of the Pacific and call into question many aspects of the colonial project.

"The Trader's Wife," set on the island of Abaiang in the Gilbert Group, is one story that provides an example. An islander kills a white trader to steal his wife, who is white and something of a rarity in the islands. He is eventually handed over to a man-of-war for punishment, after the captain threatens a naval bombardment of the village and to hang some chiefs he has seized as hostages. A fellow trader, perhaps wanting to ensure his own safety, urges that the captain should have the man shot on shore as an example to the other islanders, rather than hanging him on board the ship. In the belief that the local chiefs will carry out the execution on shore in the trader's presence, the captain consents. However, the trader carries out the execution himself by having the culprit strapped to a cannon and blasted to pieces. The story ends when the trader's dog deposits "a gory lump of horror at his master's feet" while he is eating his dinner (1898: 159). This typical Becke story portrays the relations of the colonial periphery ambiguously, illustrating in a grotesque fashion that the trader is little different from the islander in his savage violence.

The fluidity of Becke's texts is partly realized by employing contrasting images of nobility and ignobility. At times the noble savage is contrasted with the ignoble white; at others the ignoble savage is contrasted with the noble white. The movement between these images suggests that white and black are not determined and immutable categories but belong in one hierarchy

133

of civilization, and that movement up and down that hierarchy is possible. It is in this sense that Becke's texts appear ambivalent. On the one hand, they subvert many of the essentialist assumptions about race by showing that racial boundaries are not clearly demarcated, for, just as progress toward civilization is a possibility, so is regress toward savagery. On the other hand, in the subversion of racial essentialism, his texts reiterate the language of race as a component of a universalizing narrative of progress (and regress).

Because they range over such a wide geographic and cultural landscape, it might be expected that Becke's Pacific tales would acknowledge the cultural diversity of the area. However, he repeats many of the prevailing images and typifications of Pacific islanders, for example, the common racial hierarchy that posits the peoples of the Eastern Pacific as superior to those of the Western Pacific, a view that had wide currency in nineteenth-century anthropological and scientific writings and in popular texts.[11] In this view, the peoples of the area that today is referred to as Polynesia, including Hawaii, Samoa, Tonga, and Fiji, were deemed superior to the peoples of the area that we now call Melanesia, including New Guinea, New Britain, New Hebrides, and the Solomon Islands. Throughout his writings Becke reproduces these racialist discourses with his own inflections and biases. Many of his tales present the image of the brave, fearless, skillful, and noble Polynesian who, despite some negative qualities, is generally esteemed. An example is his description of the Samoan missionary stationed on the island of Nanomanga: "He was intended by nature to be a warrior, a leader of men; or—and no higher praise can I give to his dauntless courage—a boat-header on a sperm whaler. Strong of arm and quick of eye, he was the very man to either throw the harpoon or deal the death-giving thrust of the lance to the monarch of the ocean world; but fate or circumstance had made him a missionary instead. He was a fairly good missionary, but a better fisherman" (1901a: 111).

Although Becke laments the fact that this man is a missionary, he portrays a "natural man," Rousseau's "man in the state nature," whose resourcefulness, strength, agility, and courage make him perfectly attuned to life in the islands. Other images reinforce the noble nature of the Polynesian. One people in the Paumotu (Taumotu) Group in the southeastern Pacific is described as "one of the proudest, most self-reliant, and brave of any of the Polynesian race, or their offshoots" (1902: 175). While the image of the Polynesian man is one of courage and bravery, the image of the Polynesian woman is one of seductive beauty. In the story "Collier: 'The Blackbirder'" this beauty is contrasted with the violence of the labor trade.[12] Here, one of

Becke's alter egos, Tom Denison, describes his encounter with the Tahitian lover of a shipmate in highly erotic language. He focuses on the eyes, writing that her "dark, melting eyes" were glowing as a result of her lover's return. Denison thinks how lucky is his shipmate and "this dark-faced daughter of the blue Pacific to be the most witching little creature he had ever seen in all his ocean wanderings" (1897a: 163). The beauty here is beguiling and be-witching, casting a magic spell over those men who gaze upon it. The image is one of being captured against one's will and better judgment. Similar kinds of eroticization of women's bodies occur in other stories; for example, a woman of Samoa is described as "a splendidly formed young woman, with perfectly oval features and a wealth of long silken hair" (1897a: 180). Yet another story about Samoa repeats a similar description; in this case the woman is said to be "scarcely out of her girlhood" and "possessed to a very great degree all that beauty of face and figure and vivacity of expression that are met with in the Malayo-Polynesian races of the Pacific Islands" (1897a: 148). So, Becke's images of Polynesian women repeat familiar Western dis-courses from Bougainville to Michener, presenting the women as objects of male erotic desire.

In contrast to the image of the noble and beautiful Polynesians, the Mela-nesians of Becke's stories are presented in almost entirely negative terms. The dominant picture is of bloodthirsty and treacherous cannibals, with few, if any, redeeming features—that is, the ignoble savage. As suggested below, some Melanesians are so thoroughly bad that only a "few words" are needed to typify them: "As for the natives of New Britain, a few words will suffice. They were the most unmitigated savages, cowardly and treach-erous, and with the exception of the people of the villages in the vicinity of Blanche Bay, whose women wore a scanty girdle of leaves of the plant Cordyline terminalis, they passed their lives in a state of stark nudity" (1899: 194). The Melanesian man is "cowardly and treacherous," unlike the brave and noble Polynesian. The women, too, are portrayed in negative contrast to their Polynesian counterparts. The women of New Britain have no be-guiling beauty; rather than their bodies being eroticized, their nakedness is seen as a sign of primitiveness. Places such as New Britain, where Becke was a trader for a short time, are also characterized by an unhealthy envi-ronment that is likely to kill the white colonizer. If this does not occur, he will probably be eaten: "If you don't die of fever you're pretty sure to get knocked on the head and go down the nigger's gullets," Becke writes in one story (Becke and Jeffery 1901: 127). In another story set in New Britain, the inhabitants are described as "fierce and treacherous" and "more or less addicted to cannibalism" (1899: 135).

The peoples of the Equatorial Pacific are given an equivocal position in the racial hierarchy. On the one hand, the Ellice Islanders, like the Polynesians, are represented sympathetically, as noble rather than ignoble. In one story, for example, the Ellice Islanders are described as having a "gentle nature and amiable character" (1898: 106). Like the image of the Polynesian man as a fine fisherman, the Ellice Islanders are applauded for their fishing skills. As Becke says, "From morn till night the frail canoes of these semi-nude, brown-skinned, and fearless toilers of the sea may be seen by the voyager paddling swiftly over the rolling swell of the wide Pacific" (1901a: 149). On the other hand, the Gilbert Islanders are represented as more akin to the Melanesians, as ignoble rather than noble. Invariably, the Gilbert Islanders are described as a "noisy, intractable lot of devils" (1967: 52), as "fierce, wild-eyed, black-haired natives" (82), or as "wild and intractable natives" (1901a: 109). As in many of his accounts, a description of an individual suffices for a whole people: "These two men were like nearly all the people of the Kingsmill Group [Gilbert Islands]—dark-skinned, strongly built, and with a certain fierceness of visage, born of their warlike and quarrelsome nature, and which never leaves them, even in their old age" (1902: 178). Rather than their inclination to attack whites being born of a history of violent encounters with them, as Macdonald (1982: 23) has suggested, the Gilbert Islanders are considered to have a naturally violent nature. Elsewhere their violence is depicted as almost bestial: "the Gilbert Islander, whose inborn fighting proclivities were showing in his gleaming eyes and short, panting breaths" (1902: 210).

"Going Native"

It is in applying to whites the contrasting images of nobility and ignobility that Becke subverts the view of a fixed racial and civilizational hierarchy. His texts are laden with examples of black savagery, but the whites can also reach those depths, and even surpass them. In this sense, the negative representations of the blacks serve to show how far the whites have transgressed racial and cultural boundaries.

At its most rudimentary, "going native" in Becke's stories sometimes consists merely of living on an island in a thatched hut, eating the local food, and dressing as the locals do. Sometimes the whites have acquired various local skills, such as climbing coconut palms or catching bonito. However, "going native" often goes beyond these surface trappings to a more fundamental change of being—to living, behaving, and thinking as the natives do. Some men, "[c]asting away the garb of civilisation and tying around their loins the . . . grass girdle . . . soon became in appearance, manners, language, and thoughts pure natives" (Becke 1895b: 161).

Occasionally, Becke's main white character is a lone man, living on an island and married to a local woman. More typically, there are several whites living on the same island and married to local women. Often they have more than one wife, and many have what is described in one story as an "ample harem." Licentiousness is a common character trait of many of the whites he features. In the story "Hickson: A Half-Caste," Becke describes the crews of the American whaling fleet meeting at Ponape as "savagely licentious" (1895b: 119). These stories convey the archetypal image of savagery as a state of amorality where passions are totally unrestrained, and where excessive lust, violence, and greed are standard behaviors. This is a world of primitive excess, where the white traders and settlers succumb to the immoderation usually attributed to the islanders.

Often the whites have come to look like the locals, with darkened skins and tattooed bodies, as the following description suggests: "Both men were dressed like natives, naked to the waist, and save where their girdles of ti leaves protected their skins, their tattooed bodies and limbs were darkened as deeply by the rays of a tropic sun as were those of their native associates" (1897a[1987]: 146). Racial and cultural identity is sometimes blurred to such an extent that other whites are unable to discern the difference between the white "savage" and the black "savage." In the story "An Honour to the Service" (1895b), a white character has gone native to such a degree that he is mistaken for a local chief by whites visiting the island. Even his father, a member of the crew, does not recognize him. To live for a prolonged time without contact with other whites in the midst of the Pacific islanders is to risk forgetting one's identity as a white, to become one of the locals. Toward the end of the story, after being flogged for striking the captain of a ship, this man proclaims that it is years since "I saw a white man, an' I've almost forgotten I *was* a white man once" (291). Of course all travelers to foreign lands must to some extent adopt some of the lifestyle of the local inhabitants, such as eating the food, wearing the clothes, and living in local accommodations (Brantlinger 1988: 192). The point, however, is the particular way this is construed in these accounts. The adoption of the clothing and appearance of the Pacific islanders, or what Low (1993) calls cultural cross-dressing, is not a matter of practicality or a subterfuge to infiltrate indigenous societies for purposes of governance, a theme apparent in some of Kipling's tales (see Kipling 1991: 24–29). In Becke's stories, the adoption of the customs of the other is depicted as a much deeper act. It is the adoption of an inferior form of morality and lifestyle; it is to *be* different and inferior, to *be* a savage, and is thus a process of cultural and moral degeneration.

Becke's stories present life in the Pacific as precarious and dangerous, a place where one cannot retain one's cultural and racial identity without considerable and sustained effort and where one can easily give way to the "dark" forces within. He describes "going native" as a process of moral and social degeneration in which the whites descend into a savagery that is often more ugly and morally repugnant than the treachery of the Melanesians or the intractability of the Gilbert Islanders. Becke gives the reader images of the colonist's nightmare, the Kurtzian horror of *Heart of Darkness*.

Usually the whites in Becke's stories are characterized by drunkenness and brutality and, as we discuss later, they often meet a violent death. Many are in the service of local chiefs as mercenaries and in one story are referred to as "fighting-cocks" because they often participate in the warfare between groups, utilized for their fighting skills and competence with new forms of weaponry, such as muskets and rifles. This association between white and black often sees white pitted against white, and Becke's stories abound with whites killing one another in local wars or in acts of treachery and revenge. Theirs is a world of passions out of control, of desire unrestrained, an image usually ascribed to the ignoble other.

Although the actions of ignoble Pacific islanders are not usually as vile as the "white savages," Becke uses similar terms to describe both, such as "rude," "uncultured," "treacherous," "ferocious," "monster," "savage," "tiger in human form," and "shameless degraded beings." The acts whites perform in the Pacific are often considered "darker" than any they have performed in their previous lives, showing the extent to which the Pacific is a place where people lose their reason and allow their passions to run riot. In one story Becke remarks that the locals are "[l]ess cruel and treacherous than their white associates" (1897a[1987]: 73). Henry Deschard, a character who has spent many years roaming the islands of the Pacific escaping retribution for a crime, is described as "darker than the Kurians themselves" and, in "his love of the bloodshed and slaughter that so often ran riot in native quarrels," Becke writes, "he surpassed even the fiercest native"

(1895b: 163). By using the same primitivist language to represent both colonizer and colonized, the stories allude tellingly to one of the tensions of the colonial venture: the dangerous extent of the colonizers' fallibility in foreign lands. Instead of demonstrating the superiority of the colonizers, the white traders and settlers succumb to the excesses usually attributed to their "inferiors."

The story "Prescott of Naura" illustrates this theme. This story is set on Naura, an island near the Marshall Islands, known to the white traders and seamen who visit it as Pleasant Island, although, from Becke's description, pleasant it is not. The narrator immediately represents it as a wild place, inhabited by "a teeming population of noisy, intractable savages" (1897a[1987]: 65). An escaped convict, Robert Prescott, described as having a "most ferocious courage and cruel nature" and "savage spirit" (67), lands here. He and an accomplice, at Prescott's behest, poison a number of their compatriots, who all die in excruciating pain. Illustrating the great depths to which the whites have fallen, Becke writes that the local people, on hearing the agonized groans, are moved to pity, and ask the two white men to put an end to the misery. But the two villains have no pity and leave their victims to a lingering death. Even the notoriously "wild" Pleasant Islanders are filled with horror at the actions of Prescott and his accomplice, and both villains are forced off the island.

The theme of a white "savagery" that exceeds that of the islanders is also a dominant motif in "Martin of Nitendi." This story describes the acts of piracy of a white man living among an island people who attack and plunder a passing ship. Because of his acts of "reckless courage," this man is accepted into the local society and achieves a measure of authority and influence that is surpassed only by the chief. As in many stories, he has assumed "native garb" and wears a girdle of *ti* leaves and nothing else other than a hat made of coconut leaves shading his "blood-shot" and "savage" eyes from the sun. This character, Jim Martin, was put ashore by a whaling vessel because of his mutinous conduct, and as a result he has dissociated himself forever from civilization, becoming one of the most desperate and blood-stained beachcombers that had "ever cursed the fair isles of the South Pacific" (1901b: 103). Becke emphasizes that Martin's previous identity as a white man has been erased when he writes "he had been a White Man" (101). Elsewhere, again emphasizing the "savage" state to which Martin has fallen, Becke describes him as a "wild, naked creature" (102), a description that also calls into question his humanity. He had indeed become "more a savage native than a white man" (105). The story ends with a punitive expedition in pursuit of Martin for the massacre of a ship's crew. He escapes into the mountains but is eventually shot and mortally wounded by a soldier who had thought he was a "nigger." When Martin is found wounded by the lake, his racial identity is called into question when a soldier asks him, "Who are you? Are you a white man?" (111).

Of course not all the characters in Becke's Pacific tales "go native," and when they do they do not necessarily descend to such extremes of violence. Sometimes, there is a white who has "gone native" but has not succumbed to the degenerate state of brutality of the vast majority of the other white characters. In the story "In the Old, Beach-Combing Days," there is Charles Westall, who, "Unlike many of his class," was "neither a drunkard nor a ruffian" (1897a[1987]: 27). Although Westall has not "gone native" in the typical ways, he has done so in others. In the custom of the locals, he is polygamous, with five wives and twenty to thirty children (27). Another story tells of the madness of the captain of a whaling ship, a fanatically religious New Englander, who is stranded in Ponape after his crew has deserted. After living alone and hermit-like on his ship for a year, a sudden change in his "character and conduct" takes place. Going ashore, he returns with five or six women whom he keeps permanently aboard, keeping his "harem in luxury" by stripping off and selling parts of the ship, such as the sails (1895b: 122). By the end of the year the boat was stripped, and the once fanatically religious New Englander "went utterly, hopelessly mad" (122).

If the possibility of regression is an ever-present reality for those whites who live in the racial and cultural borderlands of the Pacific, then the possibility of redemption for those fallen characters is less possible. Once a white man has "gone native," the likelihood of his return to "civilization" is very limited, if not impossible. Usually the story ends in violent death, or the continuation of that life as a "native." As with Wiltshire in Stevenson's *The Beach of Falesa*, who remarks that he is "stuck here," many of Becke's characters are unable to escape the Pacific once they have fallen. The process of degeneration is, thus, conceived as a one-way journey. This is put most tellingly in one of Becke's stories when a white mercenary for a local chief, after seeing a fellow mercenary killed in an affray, in a sad echo of Walker's words to his mother ponders the future and asks quixotically of another beachcomber whether they will meet the same fate: "I wonder if you an' me is going to get finished off like poor Tommy Lane? Or is you an' me goin' to spend all our lives here among a race o' savages, livin' like 'em, thinkin' like em', and dyin' like 'em?" (1897a[1987]: 145).

As the beachcomber's words suggest, once one has "gone native" there is no alternative but to remain thus or die. Once the racial divide has been crossed there is rarely any return to "civilization," and most of the characters in Becke's stories, as Brantlinger has remarked, remain "stranded in the backwaters of Empire with nowhere to go" (1988: 41). For others who do not meet with the treacherous and violent deaths that they have often meted out to others, there is a restless wandering, in which the perpetrators of abhorrent acts spend their lives hoping their pasts will not catch up with them. The notorious Prescott, for example, spends the rest of his life as an exile, estranged from both the world into which he was born and the world into which he has fallen, unable to escape his "black past" (1897a[1987]: 79).

Unlike many of Becke's stories, where there is rarely an explanation for the fall of men apart from their presence in the Pacific, Martin's "vicious nature" is partly explained by his upbringing in the convict system, which Becke describes as "awful." Both his mother and father had been convicts and he grew up under the shadow of the gallows and the "cat" (whip). From convict to "savagery," the step, we are told, is not great: "From the simple, loafing beachcomber stage of life to that of a leader of the natives in their tribal wars was a simple but natural transition, and Jim Martin, son of a convict father and mother whose forbears were of the scum of Liverpool, and knew the prison better than the open air, followed the path ordained by Fate" (1901b: 113). This passage is of particular interest because of its inflection of the racial discourse of degeneration with a class dimension. For a lower-class person, whose forbears were the "scum of Liverpool," the fall is not so great or profound, but a fairly simple and natural transition. A similar theme is evident in the story "Prescott of Naura" mentioned above. Although many of Prescott's acts are explained by his presence in the Pacific, they are also partly explained by his experiences of the penal system at Port Arthur. "The cat took all of the white man out of me at Port Arthur," he says, "and for fifty years I lived with kanakas, and I am a kanaka now—backbone and soul" (1897a[1987]: 85). This also illustrates that it is much more likely that those who "go native" are those whose position in the class hierarchy is lowest.[13]

As Cooper and Stoler (1989: 614) have remarked, students of imperialism have discussed class issues in two ways: either by examining the nature of accumulation by the metropolitan capitalist classes, or by examining the emergence of class among the colonized set in motion by capitalist intrusion. However, as they suggest, "class impinged in the making of empire in other ways: constraining who came to the colonies, what class visions they harbored, what features of European class culture were selectively reworked . . . and ultimately how racial boundaries were maintained" (614–15). Only those of a certain class—the class to which Becke attaches himself—are capable of living and working in the Pacific without "going native." Just as Becke supports the maintenance of racial boundaries, he supports the maintenance of class boundaries. Only members of certain classes are considered to have the moral fortitude and respectability to resist the temptations to excess that the Pacific offers in the Western imagination.

Thus, Becke's stories can be read as allegories cautioning travelers and colonizers to be wary when they enter the realm of the "primitive," warning of the danger of transgressing the racial divide. To all those who do not have the right class position and sufficient masculine character, they serve as a warning to be wary.[14]

"Manliness"

Occasionally Becke's stories feature men who personify the requisite characteristics and do not fall. One such figure is Henry Lefrancois, who, writes Becke, despite his French name is English to the backbone. In an act of heroism worthy of the empire, Lefrancois first kills two treacherous men who had slaughtered an entire ship's crew in an attempt to steal its valuables and cargo, and then single-handedly sails the ship to safety. Later he settles in Hawaii, where he gains the respect of both natives and Europeans for his "sterling, straightforward character, courage, and all-round manliness of disposition" (1905: 267). It is these attributes that make this man noble, a colonist of character who, far from falling in the Pacific, proves himself. Unlike the unfortunate and pious New Englander mentioned above, who fell despite having sufficient "character and conduct," Lefrancois does not fall. Character and conduct as class-based virtues are not enough in themselves, but must be supplemented with other virtues, particularly manliness.

Becke's humorous stories featuring Tom Denison, his alter ego, and Saunderson provide additional evidence of this. Saunderson is a partner in the firm that owns the ship on which Denison is supercargo, and features in the stories "Saunderson and the Dynamite," "Saunderson and the Devilfish," and "Denison Gets Even with Saunderson." Saunderson is the type of person who has finely developed the art of annoying people. To the chagrin of others, he is not averse to telling people how to do their work, and his ineptitude lands him constantly in trouble. As Becke writes: "he was a fearful bore, a great intermeddler with other people's affairs, and was always getting himself into trouble over his officiousness, and then blaming Denison" (1967: 167). He annoys Denison by suggesting that the job of supercargo is superfluous. Despite his bourgeois position and pious nature, it would seem that he does not have the requisite character to be a successful colonizer. Saunderson fails because he lacks the "courage, and all-round manliness of disposition" of Lefrancois, an attribute that has been strengthened through long practical experience. Far from having a long history of working in the Pacific, which would have tried and tested his masculinity, making him a better man, Saunderson has only the experience of two brief voyages. Far from his actions being governed by the masculine virtues of courage and self-control, they are governed by impetuousness and stupidity, as Becke's accounts of him humorously show. Through such characters as Saunderson and others who "go native," Becke authors himself in his fiction as one who manfully maintains his cultural and racial identity and integrity.

Through the third-person voice of the narrator, Becke distances, and so fashions, himself as different from these "white natives." He writes predominantly from a position of ethnocentric and moral superiority, as one who personifies the virtues of the colonial entrepreneur, having both the requisite "character and conduct" and the "manliness of disposition" to negotiate the morally and physically testing environment he construes the Pacific to be. As in his letters, he represents himself as being willing to take risks, able to take adversity in his stride, and having the moral and physical fortitude to withstand the temptations to fall.

When he features in the stories directly through an authorial "I" he represents himself as a colonist with the ideal character and type of masculinity. An example of this is his account of his stay on Kusaie, in which he distances himself from "Bully" Hayes, whose treatment of the local inhabitants he abhors. Further, when he adopts the pseudonym of Tom Denison, the substance of the stories is often significantly different from his tales of fallen whites. Many of these stories are humorous and present a less "dark" side of the colonial venture.

Emerging from the context of the imperial expansion of the late nineteenth century, Becke's Pacific tales speak candidly of the imperial and colonial venture, articulating a counterdiscourse that suggests that the colonizing venture was not exactly the triumph portrayed by imperial history, but was fraught with contradictions. Walker's letters also speak poignantly of the failures of the colonial venture. They record a succession of economic failures much like Becke's, and foreshadow his own pathetic death in the cause of colonial trade. Neither Walker nor Becke gives us a picture of the successes of the civilizing mission.

Walker instead exposes the problematic nature of what Pratt (1992) has called the contact zone, that colonial space where cultures meet and interact. His letters suggest that the contact zone is a place of instability not only for the colonizers but for the colonized as well. When he writes that those "savages" who have been to the "white man's country" are the "biggest rogues," he is suggesting that if the colonizers are physically and morally corrupted by their sojourns in the tropics, a similar thing happens to the colonized who journey in the opposite direction. The "savage" in this view is not redeemed and elevated from his morally fallen state by his contact with the "civilized" world, as missionary narratives hold, but is corrupted by the encounter. Repeating the view that movement from one's proper place opens the potential for moral degeneration, this is a reassertion of a racial hierarchy and a statement that the colonized should stay where they are — at the bottom. Despite his occasional sympathy for those local people suffering from the harshness of the labor trade or his affection for the boy who does his domestic labor, Walker's writings speak for the colonial venture and the ideas of racial hierarchy on which it is founded. Nevertheless, though a supporter of colonialism, his writings undermine the colonial venture by narrating a dissonant tale of failure.

We have suggested that in their writings Walker and Becke articulate some of the contradictions of colonial discourse and thought. These go far beyond the economic failures they both experienced, to enunciate the view that the colonizing culture is threatened and called into question in zones of intercultural contact. If the world of the primitive other is constructed in the wider colonial discourse as a place to which people journey in search of adventure, pleasure, or profit, then the writings of Becke and Walker suggest that such journeys are not without risk. Similarly, if the space of the primitive other is constituted as the testing ground for character, where, through acts of "derring do," the masculine self is realized, then the writings of Walker and Becke illustrate that this, too, is not without risk and danger. Although it was desirable to travel to the place of the primitive other, there was the possibility that one could fall, to become like that other. Thus if, as Stoler and Cooper have recently argued, a basic tension of empire is "that the otherness of the colonised persons was neither inherent nor stable" (1997: 7) and had to be defined and maintained, this also pertains to the colonizer. As we have shown, this is evident in the writings of Walker and Becke, who present a vision of the colonizing venture always on the verge of rupture and the colonizers struggling to maintain their racial and cultural identity, which is constantly called into question and challenged. Thus, on the one hand, when Walker writes that he is becoming unfit to return home he is articulating a view that his identity as a colonizer has been called into question, that he has been debased by the colonial venture to the level of the colonized. Becke, on the other hand, protects himself from this dreadful possibility of "going native" by writing himself as a colonist with character rather than as a bad colonist.

The similarities between Becke's and Walker's experiences in the Pacific are striking. Both wrote to their mothers at contemporaneous times, both worked as traders and supercargoes, both were shipwrecked and had encounters with recalcitrant Pacific islanders. Yet there are equally remarkable differences. Despite his failures, the confident and self-assured Becke fashions himself as a good colonist through his writings. The unconfident and ineffectual Walker, on the other hand, fails to fashion himself into anything but a bad colonist. His repeated representation of himself as an "awfully bad hand" at writing epitomizes his attitude of helplessness against the tide of events and the power of others. If Becke fashions himself as an ideal type, Walker represents himself as incapable of attaining ideals. He seems unable to direct his own life toward a chosen end, and instead remains a helpless victim of circumstance, to an extent that readers may find exasperating. Paradoxically, however, his very inability to write and his very helplessness amount to a gift: for readers more than a century later, his letters enable us to understand the most glorious moment of empire from the vantage point of the poor white, which has generally been obscured by imperialist and anti-imperialist narratives alike. Walker shows the project, albeit inadvertently, as a struggle that was as futile as it was harsh.

The posthumous life of Louis Becke could be seen as a continuation of the lapse into obscurity that marked the writer's last years. It is true that his books, frequently reissued in the first decades of the twentieth century, have not totally disappeared from view. One of his best collections, *By Reef and Palm* (1894), was reprinted in 1955 and 1970; one set was translated into German in the 1960s; and another collection appeared in facsimile as recently as the late 1980s. Yet his readership is hardly the broad one that he once enjoyed. He is known, not so much to those looking simply for an adventurous tale, but to those with an interest, and probably an academic interest, in Australian literary studies. His place in history lies in short to medium-length entries in reference works such as *The Oxford Companion to Australian Literature* and the *Australian Dictionary of Biography,* as well as in A. Grove Day's (1967) fairly pedestrian commentaries. It is highly likely that he is now read and cited most frequently by those engaged in the critique of colonial fiction, such as Robert Dixon (1995) and ourselves. Only those concerned with the deconstruction of imperial culture, it seems, are concerned to keep this particular author of imperialist fantasy alive.

If Becke has a small place in history, one might think that Vernon Lee Walker has none at all. He certainly has no place in public historical consciousness in Australia or anywhere else; he scarcely figures even in the published corpus of specialist scholarly history on the Pacific islands, outside a couple of passing references (e.g., Scarr 1990: 145). Yet he once figured in a private, familial historical imagining. His niece, Helen Maria Williams, resident in Western Australia, wrote to the historian John Cumpston in the early 1960s about a trip she had made to Vanuatu, then the New Hebrides. It seems that she had gone, principally, in order to make some kind of contact with the place in which her uncles had worked, and where Lee had died, even though she did not travel to Pentecost itself.

> Visited New Hebrides in June of this year. Received with hospitality by the Newman family, going first of all to Oscar Newman at Tisman on Malekula. Was taken to Port Sandwich, where, in pouring rain and such humidity as I had never before encountered, I found the old aban-

doned Soldier's cemetary in which Uncle Lee had been buried—the whole gloomy place undermined with land crabs down whose holes I fell repeatedly . . .

While staying with Olive and Stan Breusch at Oaba [Aoba, now Ambae], a native from Pentecost related the story of the murder which had been passed on to him by his father—also sang a song made up about it which he said was still sung and danced to!!! in the village. The story was as written in letters but a grisly bit added about one poor native with yaws, who could not run and hid when the soldiers came and who was taken by the soldiers, after the village was burnt, etc., and strung up the mast of the ship and shot. He also said that Lee was known and liked by the coastal tribes but it so happened that fatal morning that an inland tribe was down on shore and the chief's wives were all out on the reef collecting whatever they do collect there, when the boat rowed ashore with [the] white man standing up in it holding out some trade goods and one [of] the women made a grab at it and it looked as though she was being dragged into [the] boat and, as there had been a lot of women stealing by whaling crews going on, the chief shot him and hacked him to pieces.

In Vila, at the Joint Court, I saw records in both uncles' hand writing of the purchase and sale of land, the former, bearing the names of several natives with unpronounceable names, who were only able to put a cross against their names and who sold some 1000 acres for about £75 worth of trade goods.

This land was at Port Sandwich, on which the French Residency now stands. There did not seem to be any record of land mentioned as being owned at Pentecost. (NLA MS 904)

This fragment indicates, intriguingly, that Walker not only remained alive, in some sense, for Helen Williams, but also for some of the people of Pentecost. The man who related this account may well have added the point that Walker was liked by the locals specifically for his listener's benefit; the significance of the ancestor for the descendent would hardly have been lost on the average Melanesian. However, it is equally possible that this was true, and the rest of the narrative is entirely consistent with the kinds of antagonisms that existed between coastal and bush peoples, and with the cycles of reciprocal violence that incidents of violence and kidnapping occasioned during the years of disorderly colonial trade.

This text provides us with a glimpse of indigenous historical imagining

147

that this book has otherwise neglected. The nature of its particular inquiry has perforce confined us within the uncertainties and contradictions of a European archive. In general, we are unable to reconstruct how Becke, or the figures like Walker upon whom he based his characters, were perceived by the Fijians who dived for coins, by Noumea houseboys, or by those who engaged in trade in Micronesia and Vanuatu. It is vital to recall that there were many other perceptions of these actors, and perhaps many other ways of narrating their successes and failures. Yet, if the composition of this book has been dogged by a lingering concern that we are rehabilitating bad colonists, it is just possible that Vernon Lee Walker has, over the past hundred years, figured in indigenous histories in ways that he could not have anticipated and that we cannot now reconstruct.

❧ Notes

Introduction

1   I have not ventured here to discuss cross-cultural variation in the value and use of
letters, a topic discussed in an exemplary manner by Besnier (1995: chs. 4 and 5).
Although his discussion is most illuminating concerning the specific investments in
letters in Nukulaelae (a Polynesian atoll) culture, some of the points he makes are
more widely suggestive: "Events like letter writing and reading on Nukulaelae thus
hypercognize affect: emotions are referred to more overtly and frequently than in
other communicative events"; "Nukulaelae Islanders *define* letter writing and reading
as affectively cathartic contexts, in which certain types of emotions are hypercog-
nized"(111).

1. "An Awfully Bad Hand at Letter Writing": Vernon Lee Walker
and Colonial History

1   For general background, see Scarr (1967) and Howe (1984), and on labor recruiting
specifically, Corris (1973), Moore (1985), and Jolly (1987). These include citations to
many primary texts and publications of the period that incorporate much richer descriptions of trading and labor recruiting than Walker's.

2. The Letters of Vernon Lee Walker, 1878–1887

1   Walker's punctuation is idiosyncratic. Instead of a full stop he usually uses a somewhat decorative mark which looks like an equal sign. These have been replaced with
full stops throughout his letters.

2   Note written on page: "Lee was killed Dec 21st, 1887. Cyril W. Walker."

3   Margin Note: "Lee was killed on 21st and buried on 22nd."
     Newspaper clipping pinned to page 3 with handwritten note: "Cutting from Keble's
Margate and Ramsgate Gazette.—dated 16 Feb 1889":

     —MURDER OF EUROPEANS IN THE SOUTH SEAS.
     According to advice received on Monday from New Zealand, her Majesty's ship
Opal returned to Auckland at the end of December from a cruise among the islands
of the South Seas, the natives of which had murdered a number of Europeans. The
Opal ascertained at Apia that no fewer than four persons had recently been murdered and then mutilated. One of these was a Swede, and a second a French half
caste. Three of the murdered men were first cast ashore, their boat having capsized.
On arrival at Port Sandwich it was found that the natives had made a murderous

attack on a Queensland trading vessel, and that the Government agent, a Mr Cecil, had received most serious wounds. Prior to taking any action here, it was decided to proceed to Pentecost Island, where a Mr Vernon Lee Walker and a boat's crew had been treacherously murdered. A friendly chief afforded the required information as to the guilty tribe, and the chief of the offending natives was forthwith summoned to come on board the Opal, and pay the penalty of his misdeeds, or war would be declared. In reply, the chief sent a refusal, but offered as a reparation, a man and two pigs. He next offered to give up the "actual murderer," but no notice was taken of this offer inasmuch as forty or more were concerned in the attack. The surf was heavy, and the men could not well land, but the village was bombarded, the natives flying into the bush. At Port Sandwich the Opal was joined by the French man-of-war Fabert, and each vessel, proceeding to Si, landed together 120 men. These marched to the village, the natives flying at their approach, and having burned all the huts, and destroyed all they possibly could of the plantations, returned on board. The vessels parted company here. The Opal visited Paama, and burned the village there, and then left for New Zealand.

3. Self-Fashioning and Savagery: Louis Becke's Pacific Letters

1 Louis Becke (1902: 217).
2 For studies that consider the ways the colonizers themselves were imagined, see Cooper and Stoler (1989), Eves (1998), Stoler (1989a, 1989b, 1995), and Thomas (1994).
3 Further biographical details on Becke can be found in the introduction to Day (1966, 1967, 1987), Maude (1956, 1967), and Michener and Day (1957). Discussions of his work can be found in Baird (1956), Day (1966, 1967, 1987), Dixon (1995), Ingram (1937), and Thomas (1993).
4 The supercargo was responsible for the trade store on a ship, serving to replenish the stock of land-based trade stores.
5 As noted above, the charges were dismissed, Becke having played no part in obtaining the ship.
6 In his later writings Becke presents a far more complex and informed picture of the local inhabitants, despite his use of the language of race.
7 Or what Brantlinger has referred to as "New Imperialism" (1988: ix).
8 There are, of course, also marked differences because their objectives and scope tend to vary. "The objective of autobiography is a life, not simply a record of the things which have 'touched upon' an existence," which is what letters tend to recount (Weintraub 1975: 824).

4. The Letters of Louis Becke, 1880–1882

1 According to Firth (1977: 8), after fluctuating from as high as £22 per ton at the end of the 1870s to £15 in 1881, and back to £20 in 1882, the European price of copra entered a decline from which it did not recover until 1901.

2 Scarr, for example, suggests that "The High Commissioner's success in bringing British offenders to justice was very slight indeed" (1967: 162). For a much fuller account of the difficulties of the Western Pacific High Commission in governing British subjects, see in particular Scarr (1967) and Brookes (1972: 416).

3 Though Munro is quick to dismiss the use of material deriving from Becke in relation to the trading venture of De Wolf and Company because of factual inaccuracies, he utilizes material from Becke that has come second-hand through Day.

4 Tom De Wolf, to whom Becke dedicated one of his books, and who is often mentioned in his stories, was on quite good terms with Becke and never stringently adhered to these instructions. He was evidently involved in supplying guns on credit to a group of Samoans from the Malietoa party for their wars (Munro 1980: 34). Becke, on the other hand, suggests that to help free the country "from the hated Germans," Tom De Wolf lent Malietoa a large sum of money to pay off his debt to the great German trading firm (1895a: 287). Whatever the case, it certainly illustrates that De Wolf was not averse to meddling in local politics himself.

5 Certainly from the account of Alfred Restieaux, one of the traders Becke met on Nanumea, not all of De Wolf's employees followed his strictures. The captain in charge of *The Venus* often found refuge in the bottle and was incapable of performing his duties to such an extent that the British consul in Samoa sent a telegraph to the firm's head office in London informing them of his neglect (Munro 1980: 26–27).

6 George P. Winchcombe 1881–1887, Diary, in Louis Becke Papers, Microfilm CY Reel 491 of Dixson Library Manuscript 159, ML Safe 1/8.

7 Hernsheim and Company was a trading firm established by Captain Eduard Hernsheim in the 1870s and seems to have been very successful. As Firth (1978: 115) has noted, and I am relying on his account here, Hernsheim was notable as one of the few speculative traders of any period in the Pacific islands whose commercial venture was profitable. At its height, he had trading stations in the Caroline and Marshall Islands, where his brother Franz was stationed from 1878, and in the islands of the Bismarck Archipelago, such as the Duke of York Islands, in New Ireland and New Britain, where Eduard was based. Although Becke does not specify who he had worked for in New Britain, it is very likely that it was for Hernsheim, whose trading interests there were extensive. Unlike De Wolf and Company, who sought reputable traders, Hernsheim was not so discerning. One of his agents recruited four traders in Ponape in 1877 because they were prepared to work in parts of the Pacific where few whites had ventured, but they were "all degenerate and addicted to drink, always ready for a fight and carrying a revolver" (Hernsheim cited in Firth 1978: 119).

8 On Anglo-German rivalry in the Pacific, see Knight (1977), Masterman (1934), and Scarr (1967).

9 On the German New Guinea Company, see Firth (1972). On German firms more generally in the Pacific, see Firth (1977, 1978) and Spoehr (1963).

1   This chapter heading is taken from the title of one of the reviews of Becke's collection of stories entitled *Pacific Tales*. Of course not all Becke's stories present this theme. His writings are varied and many are humorous and lighthearted.

2   Degeneration was also a common theme in the metropolitan centers of Europe in the late nineteenth century. See Bowler (1989: 196–97), Buckley (1967), Greenslade (1994), Morton (1984), Pick (1989), Siegel (1985), and Torgovnick (1990).

3   See also Stepan (1982, 1985), Stocking (1968), and Thomas (1996).

4   Degeneration is a common theme in narratives of white travel and residence in tropical lands. There are a considerable number of nonfiction accounts from the Pacific. The Methodist missionary Burton refers to some whites who lived in Fiji as "men who sank lower than the lowest savage, and found delight in deeds of blood and abhorrent cruelty" (1944: 12). In an earlier work he suggests that these whites "lived lives that out-rivalled, in filthiness and wickedness, the cannibal Fijian" (1910: 23). There is also the case of John Renton, discussed by Becke (Becke and Jeffery 1901: 101–12), Holthouse (1988), and Marwick (1935). Charles Savage, probably one of those Burton is referring to, is discussed by Davidson (1975) and by Orr (1977) in a novel based on his life. For discussions that touch on "going native" in other colonial fiction, see Brantlinger (1988), Katz (1987), Low (1993), Parry (1993: 228), and Street (1975). For discussions that explore this in relation to literature about the Pacific, such as R. M. Ballantyne's *The Coral Island*, see Street (1975), Green (1989), and Hannabuss (1989). For Robert Louis Stevenson's *The Beach of Falesa* and *The Ebb Tide*, see Brantlinger (1988: 39–42).

5   He also wrote a collection of stories from his time in France, *Sketches from Normandy*.

6   Among these are "Tarria, the Swimmer," already mentioned, and others such as "A Truly Great Man: a Mid-Pacific Sketch," "The Trader's Wife," "Chester's 'Cross,'" "Collier, the Blackbirder," and "The Shadows of the Dead." Others based in the Gilbert and Ellice Islands are "Pakia," "Solepa," "The Fisher Folk of Nukufetau," "The 'Palu' of the Equatorial Pacific," "The Rangers of the Tia Kau," "The Brothers-in-Law: A Tale of the Equatorial Islands," "The Strange Adventure of James Shervinton," "'Pig-Headed' Sailor Men," "Apinoka of Apamama," "The Fate of the Alida," "Mrs. Malleson's Rival," "The Peruvian Slavers," "A Question of Precedence," "Long Charley's Good Little Wife," and "A Hundred Fathoms Deep."

7   Such as "The Methodical Mr Burr of Majuru," "A Point of Theology on Maduro," and "The Strange White Woman of Maduro."

8   During the height of his literary career at the turn of the century he was compared favorably to Kipling, being referred to as the Kipling of the Pacific. Becke knew Kipling personally, being a neighbor of his in Eastbourne where he lived for some of his time in England. During his stay in London he was very familiar with the literary scene and often included discussion of literary figures and recent novels in his column "London Notes" in the *Sydney Evening News*. He was a great admirer of Stevenson and thought that the *Beach of Falesa*, a tale of trading life in the Pacific, was the best novel of Polynesian life since Kingsley and Pembroke's *South Sea Bubbles* (Becke 1895a). He

would undoubtedly have known of Conrad, but whether he was a source of literary inspiration is unclear. Conrad is reputed to have known and admired Becke's work (Day 1987: 7).

9 *Westminster Gazette* 30 August 1997. For more of his views on German colonialism, see Becke (1899–1900). In collaboration with Walter Jeffery, Becke also wrote a glowing account of George Grey's contribution to the British Empire (1898).

10 He refers occasionally to Germans who are "White men," meaning that they behave like whites and not blacks.

11 Having its origins in some of the writings of scientists on Cook's voyages of exploration to the South Seas in the eighteenth century, it was developed more fully by D'Urville in the early part of the nineteenth century (Thomas 1989). It was, and still is, widely deployed by anthropologists and by many of the missionaries evangelizing in the Pacific in the early part of the twentieth century (Eves 1996). This division also features in other fictional writings on the Pacific, such as those by Jack London, written at the turn of the century (Eves 1998).

12 This story is apparently based on an incident involving a labor recruiter from Fiji who, finding himself short of supplies, off-loaded eighty Gilbert Islanders onto a vessel bound for Tahiti. The Gilbert Islanders escaped from the hold, and in the ensuing fight the captain, some of the crew, and a number of the Gilbert Islanders were killed. A member of the crew blew up a section of the ship to thwart the attackers, and the surviving Gilbert Islanders swam to a nearby island (Macdonald 1982: 60 and see also Newbury 1956: 164).

13 Lombroso's criminal anthropology comes to mind here. It explains criminal behavior through the same language of race and class, saturated with ideas of regression, atavism, and degeneration. For a discussion of the primitivism in Lombroso, see Gould (1981).

14 In a number of colonies, the problem of whites "going native" was addressed by controlling immigration into the colony, as well as movement of both colonizers and colonized. For a brief discussion of this, see Eves (1998), and for a more comprehensive discussion, see Stoler (1989a, 1989b).

✿ Bibliography

Manuscripts

Becke, L. (1880–1905). Papers. Mitchell Library, State Library of New South Wales, Sydney, MS A1372–4.

—— (1880–1913). Papers. Dixson Library, State Library of New South Wales, Sydney, ML MS 248.

—— (1892). Letter to J. H. Maiden, January 12, 1892. Inwards correspondence, Powerhouse Museum, Sydney.

Walker, V. L. (1875–82). Papers. Australian Manuscript Collection, State Library of Victoria, Melbourne, MS 7568.

—— (1878–87). Letters. Rhodes House, Oxford, Mss.Pac.s.41.

Winchcombe, G. P. (1881–87). Diary, in Louis Becke Papers, Microfilm CY Reel 491 of Dixson Library Manuscript 159, ML Safe 1/8, State Library of New South Wales, Sydney.

Published Works

Baird, J. (1956). *Ishmael*. Baltimore: Johns Hopkins University Press.

Becke, L. (1894 [1955]). *By Reef and Palm*, Sydney: Angus and Robertson.

—— (1895a). "Interview. An Australasian Character Sketch: A New Australian Writer; Mr. Louis Becke." *Review of Reviews*, March 20.

—— (1895b). *The Ebbing of the Tide: South Sea Stories*. London: T. Fisher Unwin.

—— (1896a). *His Native Wife*. London: T. Fisher Unwin.

—— (1896b). "Our Lost Supremacy in the South Seas: A Chat with Mr. Louis Becke." *St. James Gazette*, August 14.

—— (1897a [1987]). *Pacific Tales*. London: Kegan Paul International.

—— (1897b). "Ema, the Half-Blood." *Town: A Magazine for the Moment*, March, 8–40.

—— (1898). *Rodman the Boatsteerer, and Other Stories*. London: T. Fisher Unwin.

—— (1899). *Ridan the Devil: And Other Stories*. London: T. Fisher Uwin.

—— (1899–1900). "The Surrender of Samoa; And How It Will Affect Missionary Enterprise." *Leisure Hour*, 218–21.

—— (1901a). *By Rock and Pool on an Austral Shore*. London: T. Fisher Unwin.

—— (1901b). *Yorke the Adventurer and Other Stories*. Philadelphia: J. B. Lippincott.

—— (1902). *The Strange Adventure of James Shervinton and Other Stories*. London: T. Fisher Unwin.

—— (1905). *Under Tropic Skies*. London: T. Fisher Unwin.

—— (1913). *The Adventures of Louis Blake*. London: T. Werner Laurie.

—— (1923). *Bully Hayes: Buccaneer and Other Stories*. Sydney: NSW Bookstall.

——— (1967). *South Sea Supercargo.* Honolulu: University of Hawaii Press.

Becke, L., and W. Jeffery (1898). "A Builder of the Empire: Sir George Grey." *Fortnightly Review,* 620–26.

——— (1901). *The Tapu of Banderah.* London: C. Arthur Pearson.

Besnier, N. (1995). *Literacy, Emotion and Authority: Reading and Writing on a Polynesian Atoll.* Cambridge: Cambridge University Press.

Bowler, P. J. (1989). *The Invention of Progress: The Victorians and the Past.* Oxford: Basil Blackwell.

Brantlinger, P. (1988). *Rule of Darkness: British Literature and Imperialism, 1830–1914.* Ithaca, NY: Cornell University Press.

Brookes, J. I. (1972). *International Rivalry in the Pacific Islands 1800–1875.* New York: Russell and Russell.

Buckley, J. H. (1967). *The Triumph of Time: A Study of the Victorian Concepts of Time, History, Progress, and Decadence.* Cambridge, MA: Harvard University Press.

Burton, J. W. (1910). *The Fiji of Today.* London: Charles H. Kelly.

——— (1944). *Brown and White in the South Pacific.* Sydney: Australian Institute of International Affairs.

Chakrabarty, D. (1994). "Embodying Freedom: Gandhi and the Body of the Public Man in India." In *Bodies,* ed. D. Walker, S. Garton, and J. Horne. Special issue of *Australian Cultural History* no. 13: 100–10.

Collini, S. (1985). "The Idea of 'Character' in Victorian Political Thought." *Transactions of the Royal Historical Society* 35: 29–50.

Cooper, F., and A. L. Stoler (1989). "Introduction. Tensions of Empire: Colonial Control and Visions of Rule." *American Ethnologist* 16(4): 609–21.

Corris, P. (1973). *Passage, Port and Plantation: A History of Solomon Islands Labour Migration, 1870–1914.* Melbourne: Melbourne University Press.

Davidson, J. W. (1975). *Peter Dillon of Vanikoro: Chevalier of the South Seas.* Melbourne: Oxford University Press.

Day, A. G. (1966). *Louis Becke.* New York: Twayne Publishers.

——— (1967). Introduction to *South Sea Supercargo,* by L. Becke. Honolulu: University of Hawaii Press, 1–11.

——— (1987). *Mad about Islands: Novelists of a Vanished Pacific.* Honolulu: Mutual Publishing Company.

Dixon, R. (1995). *Writing the Colonial Adventure: Race, Gender and Nation in Anglo-Australian Popular Fiction, 1875–1914.* Melbourne: Cambridge University Press.

Eves, R. (1996). "Colonialism, Corporeality and Character: Methodist Missions and the Refashioning of Bodies in the Pacific." *History and Anthropology* 10(1): 85–138.

——— (1998). "Going Troppo: Images of White Savagery, Degeneration and Race in Turn-of-the-Century Colonial Fictions of the Pacific." In *The Politics of Knowledge: Science and Evolution in Asia and the Pacific,* ed. M. Low and C. Dureau. Special issue of *History and Anthropology,* in press.

Field, H. J. (1982). *Towards a Programme of Imperial Life: The British Empire at the Turn of Century.* Oxford: Oxford University Press.

Firth, S. (1972). "The New Guinea Company, 1885–1899: A Case of Unprofitable Imperialism." *Historical Studies* 15: 361–77.

—— (1977). "German Firms in the Pacific Islands, 1857–1914." In *Germany in the Pacific and Far East, 1870–1914,* ed. J. A. Moses and P. M. Kennedy. St. Lucia: University of Queensland Press, 3–25.

—— (1978). "Captain Hernsheim: Pacific Venturer, Merchant Prince." In *More Pacific Islands Portraits,* ed. D. Scarr. Canberra: Australian National University Press, 115–30.

Gould, S. J. (1981). *The Mismeasure of Man.* New York: Norton.

Green, M. (1989). "The Robinson Crusoe Story." In *Imperialism and Juvenile Literature,* ed. J. Richards. Manchester: Manchester University Press, 34–52.

Greenslade, W. (1994). *Degeneration, Culture and the Novel, 1880–1940.* Cambridge: Cambridge University Press.

Hallett, L. (n.d.). "A History of Henderson and Macfarlane." Pacific Manuscripts Bureau 62. Henderson and Macfarlane, Auckland, New Zealand.

Hannabuss, S. (1989). "Ballantyne's Message of Empire." In *Imperialism and Juvenile Literature,* ed. J. Richards. Manchester: Manchester University Press, 53–71.

Holthouse, H. (1988). *White Headhunter.* Sydney: Angus and Robertson.

Howe, K. R. (1984). *Where the Waves Fall: A New South Sea Islands History from First Settlement to Colonial Rule.* Sydney: Allen and Unwin.

Ingram, M. A. (1937). "Louis Becke: A Study." M.A. Thesis, University of Hawaii.

Jolly, M. (1987). "The Forgotten Women: A History of Migrant Labour and Gender Relations in Vanuatu." *Oceania* 58 (2): 119–39.

Katz, W. R. (1987). *Rider Haggard and the Fiction of Empire: A Critical Study of British Imperial Fiction.* Cambridge: Cambridge University Press.

Kipling, R. (1991). *Plain Tales from the Hills.* Oxford: Oxford University Press.

Knight, M. P. (1977). "Britain, Germany and the Pacific, 1880–87." In *Germany in the Pacific and Far East, 1870–1914,* ed. J. A. Moses and P. M. Kennedy. St. Lucia, Queensland: University of Queensland Press, 61–88.

Low, G. C-L. (1993). "White Skins/Black Masks: The Pleasures and Politics of Imperialism." In *Space and Place: Theories of Identity and Location,* ed. E. Carter, J. Donald, and J. Squire. London: Lawrence and Wishart, 241–66.

Macdonald, B. (1982). *Cinderellas of the Empire: Towards a History of Kiribati and Tuvalu.* Canberra: Australian National University Press.

Marks, S. (1987) (ed.). *Not Either an Experimental Doll: The Separate Worlds of Three South African Women.* Bloomington: Indiana University Press.

Marwick, J. G. (1935). *The Adventures of John Renton.* Kirkwall: The Kirkwall Press.

Masterman, S. (1934). *The Origins of International Rivalry in Samoa, 1845–1884.* London: George Allen and Unwin.

Maude, H. E. (1956). "Louis Becke, 1855–1913: The Writer Who Lived His Own Pacific Romances." *Pacific Islands Monthly* 27: 87, 111, 113.

—— (1967). "Louis Becke: The Trader's Historian." Review of *Louis Becke,* by A. G. Day. *Journal of Pacific History* 2: 225–27.

Michener, J. A., and A. G. Day (1957). *Rascals in Paradise.* London: Secker and Warburg.

Mitchell, W. J. T. (1994) (ed.). *Landscape and Power.* Chicago: University of Chicago Press.

Moore, C. (1985). *Kanaka: A History of Melanesian Mackay.* Port Moresby: Institute of Papua New Guinea Studies/University of Papua New Guinea Press.

Morton, P. (1984). *The Vital Science: Biology and the Literary Imagination, 1860–1900.* London: George Allen and Unwin.

Munro, D. (1980). "Tom De Wolf's Pacific Venture: The Life History of a Commercial Enterprise in Samoa." *Pacific Studies* 3(2): 22–40.

Newbury, C. W. (1956). "The Administration of French Oceania, 1842–1906," Ph.D. thesis, Australian National University.

Orr, J. C. (1977). *Savage of Bau.* Sydney: Koa Productions.

"Papalan-hi." (1878) "A Trip to Fiji" (no. 1). *The Age,* January 19, 1878. [Subsequent parts in January 26, February 2, February 9, and February 16].

Parry, B. (1993). "The Contents and Discontents of Kipling's Imperialism." In *Space and Place: Theories of Identity and Location,* ed. E. Carter, J. Donald, and J. Squire. London: Lawrence and Wishart, 221–40.

Pick, D. (1989). *Faces of Degeneration: A European Disorder, c. 1848–1918.* Cambridge: Cambridge University Press.

Pratt, M. L. (1992). *Imperial Eyes: Travel Writing and Transculturation.* London: Routledge.

Richards, J. (1989). "With Henty to Africa." In *Imperialism and Juvenile Literature,* ed. J. Richards. Manchester: Manchester University Press, 72–106.

Scarr, D. (1967). *Fragments of Empire: A History of the Western Pacific High Commission 1877–1914.* Canberra: Australian National University Press.

——— (1990). *The History of the Pacific Islands: Kingdoms of the Reef.* Sydney: Macmillan.

Shapiro, M. J. (1988). *The Politics of Representation: Writing Practices in Biography, Photography, and Policy Analysis.* Madison: University of Wisconsin Press.

Siegel, S. (1985). "Literature and Degeneration: The Representation of 'Decadence.'" In *Degeneration: The Dark Side of Progress,* ed. J. E. Chamberlin and S. L. Gilman. New York: Columbia University Press, 199–219.

Smith, B. (1985). *European Vision and the South Seas, 1768–1850: A Study in the History of Art and Ideas.* Sydney: Harper & Row.

Spoehr, F. M. (1963). *White Falcon: The House of Godeffroy and Its Commercial and Scientific Role in the Pacific.* Palo Alto, CA: Pacific Books.

Stanley, H. M. (1890). *In Darkest Africa: Or, The Quest, Rescue and Retreat of Emin, Governor of Equatoria.* London: S. Low, Marston, Searle and Rivington.

Stepan, N. (1982). *The Idea of Race in Science: Great Britain, 1800–1960.* London: Macmillan.

——— (1985). "Biological Degeneration: Races and Proper Places." In *Degeneration: The Dark Side of Progress,* ed. J. E. Chamberlin and S. L. Gilman. New York: Columbia University Press, 97–120.

Stocking, G. W. (1968). *Race, Culture, and Evolution: Essays in the History of Anthropology.* New York: The Free Press.

Stoler, A. L. (1989a). "Making Empire Respectable: The Politics of Race and Sexual Morality in Twentieth-Century Colonial Cultures." *American Ethnologist* 16(4): 634–60.

——— (1989b). "Rethinking Colonial Categories: European Communities and the Boundaries of Rule." *Comparative Studies in Society and History* 31: 134–61.

———— (1995). *Race and the Education of Desire: Foucault's History of Sexuality and the Colonial Order of Things*. Durham, NC: Duke University Press.

Stoler, A. L., and F. Cooper (1997). "Between Metropole and Colony: Rethinking a Research Agenda." In *Tensions of Empire: Colonial Cultures in a Bourgeois World*, ed. F. Cooper and A. L. Stoler. Berkeley: University of California Press, 1–56.

Strathern, M. (1988). *The Gender of the Gift: Problems with Women and Problems with Society in Melanesia*. Berkeley: University of California Press.

Street, B. V. (1975). *The Savage in Literature: Representations of "Primitive" Society in English Fiction 1858–1920*. London: Routledge and Kegan Paul.

Thomas, N. (1989). "The Force of Ethnology: Origins and Significance of the Melanesia/ Polynesia Division." *Current Anthropology* 30(1): 27–34.

———— (1993). "The Beautiful and the Damned." In *Pirating the Pacific: Images of Travel, Trade and Tourism*, ed. A. Stephen. Sydney: Powerhouse Publishing, 44–59.

———— (1994). *Colonialism's Culture: Anthropology, Travel and Government*. Princeton, NJ: Princeton University Press.

———— (1996). " 'On the Varieties of the Human Species': Forster's Comparative Ethnology." In Johann Reinhold Forster, *Observations Made During a Voyage Round the World*, ed. N. Thomas, H. Guest, and M. Dettelbach. Honolulu: University of Hawaii Press, xxiii–xl.

Torgovnick, M. (1990). *Gone Primitive: Savage Intellects, Modern Lives*. Chicago: University of Chicago Press.

Walsh, J. M. (1982). "The Last Voyage of the 'Doravi' from Overdue." In *New Guinea Images in Australian Literature*, ed. N. Krauth. St. Lucia: University of Queensland Press, 85–92.

Watt, I. (1957). *The Rise of the Novel*. London: Chatto.

Weintraub, K. J. (1975). "Autobiography and Historical Consciousness." *Critical Inquiry* 1: 821–48.

Woodford, C. M. (1890). *A Naturalist among the Headhunters: Being an Account of Three Visits to the Solomon Islands in the Years 1886, 1887, and 1888*. London: George Philip.

Nicholas Thomas is Director of the Centre for Cross-
Cultural Research at the Australian National University.
He is the author of a number of books, including *In
Oceania: Visions, Artifacts, Histories* (Duke, 1997).
Richard Eves is an Australian Research Council
Postdoctoral Fellow in Anthropology at the Australian
National University.

Library of Congress Cataloging-in-Publication Data
Bad colonists : the South Seas letters of Vernon Lee Walker
and Louis Becke / Nicholas Thomas and Richard Eves.
Selected letters of Vernon Lee Walker and Louis Becke,
with commentary.
Includes bibliographical references and index.
ISBN 0-8223-2257-9 (cloth : alk. paper).
ISBN 0-8223-2222-6 (paper : alk. paper)
1. Oceania—History—Sources.   2. Walker, Vernon Lee—
Homes and haunts—Oceania.   3. Becke, Louis, 1855–
1913—Homes and haunts—Oceania.   I. Walker, Vernon
Lee.   II. Becke, Louis, 1855–1913.   III. Thomas,
Nicholas.   IV. Eves, Richard.
DU18.B33   1999   995—dc21   98-21598   CIP